PRINCE SHIPS OF NORTHERN B.C.

Ships of the Grand Trunk Pacific and Canadian National Railways

The dining room of the *Prince Rupert*.

Norman Hacking

PHOTO CREDITS
B. C. Ferries: 66; Canadian National Information Services: 6, 51;
Prince Rupert City and Regional Archives: 18-19, 21, 33, 34 (bottom),
39; Provincial Archives of B. C.: 9 (bottom), 31 (top), 34 (top), 37,
51 (bottom), 57, 59, 60; Public Archives of Canada: 9 (top), 10, 11, 12,
36; Vancouver Maritime Museum: 14-15, 17, 23, 24, 26, 28, 29,
31 (bottom), 40-41, 45, 48-49, 56; World Ship Society: Front Cover.

Canadian Cataloguing in Publication Data

Hacking, Norman R., 1912-
  The Prince ships of Northern B. C.

  Includes bibliographical references and index.
  ISBN 1-895811-28-7

  1. Coastwise shipping – British Columbia – History. 2.
Steamship lines – British Columbia – History. 3. Grand Trunk
Pacific Railway – History. 4. Canadian National Railways –
History. I. Title.
HE770.H34 1995   387.5'24'09711   C95-910045-8

First Edition – 1995

HERITAGE HOUSE PUBLISHING COMPANY LTD.
Unit #8, 17921 55th Ave., Surrey, B. C., V3S 6C4

Printed in Canada

Contents

The Author

Norman Hacking was born in Vancouver, graduated in history at the University of British Columbia, and was for 30 years marine editor of the *Vancouver Daily Province*. He is an honorary commodore of the Port of Vancouver, and received the Medal of Merit for marine writing in 1979 from the Canadian Port and Harbour Association.

He is the author of many articles on marine subjects, and his books include *The Princess Story: A Century and a Half of West Coast Shipping,* with W. Kaye Lamb; *The Two Barneys: A Nostalgic Memoir about Two Great British Columbia Seamen;* and *Captain William Moore: B. C.'s Amazing Frontiersman.* During World War Two he served for four years on the North Atlantic with the Royal Canadian Navy.

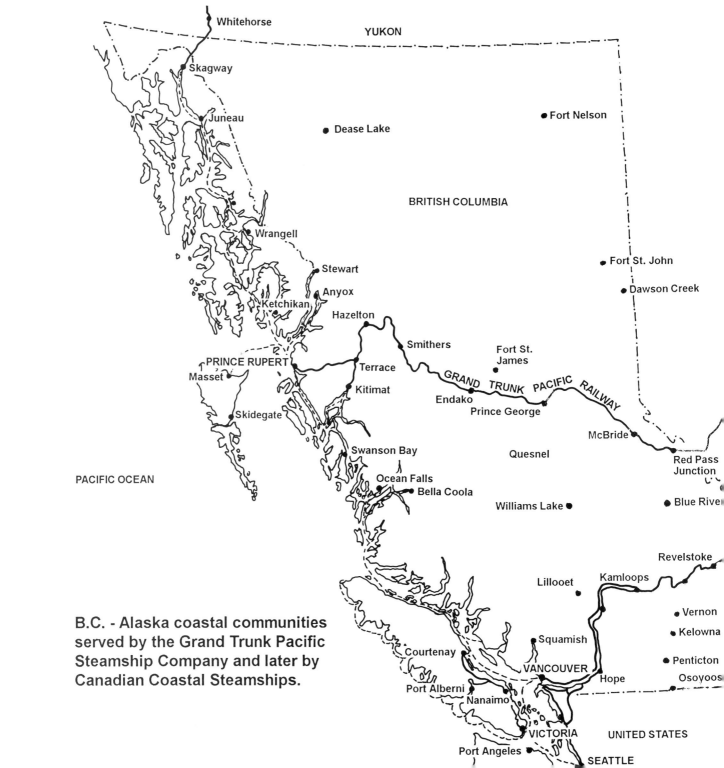

B.C. - Alaska coastal communities served by the Grand Trunk Pacific Steamship Company and later by Canadian Coastal Steamships.

CHAPTER ONE

Rocks, Muskeg, and Rain

For 65 years from 1910 to 1975 several of the finest coastwise passenger liners ever to sail in North American waters operated on the British Columbia coast from Vancouver to the ports of Prince Rupert and southeastern Alaska. They were the Princes of the North, beginning with the graceful three-funnelled *Prince Rupert* and *Prince George* in 1910 and ending when the second *Prince George* was withdrawn from service in 1975.

Operated first by the ill-fated Grand Trunk Pacific Steamship Company, and later by Canadian National Steamship Company Ltd., they were superceded by the advent of air services and modern highways. Their memory is cherished by many old-timers who recall with nostalgia the comfortable old-fashioned service they provided. They are especially revered in Prince Rupert, the city they helped to establish.

Prince Rupert on British Columbia's northern coast is today a thriving city of some 17,000. It is an important seaport, with multi-thousand-ton freighters loading coal, grain, lumber and pulp for the markets of the world. It is also a southern terminus of the Alaska State Ferry System and the northern terminus of B.C. Ferries.

Would it, in addition, have been a community to rival Vancouver if an iceberg in the North Atlantic hadn't interceded? Probably not. But it undoubtedly would have been many times larger than today.

Its story began on the morning of May 17, 1906, when surveyors approached a 28-square-mile rocky island called Kaien (pronounced KAY-an), chosen to become the terminus of a Canadian transcontinental railway and a major seaport. Kaien was 40 miles south of the Alaska border, aptly described as nothing but "Rocks, Muskeg and Rain." It did, however, have one major quality — an excellent harbour.

But as the surveyors approached the west shore of the Island that May day, they probably weren't impressed with the harbour, however grand. It was raining — not unusual since the average rainfall is 96 inches a year — and the bush which grew thickly down to the water's edge was dripping wet and the ground soggy. This modest activity was the beginning of a national dream, the construction of the western terminus of Canada's new Grand Trunk Pacific Railway.

The dreamer was a sturdy American, Charles Melville Hays, president of the Grand Trunk. He had personally chosen the site as the only possible location in the area for his great seaport. Now comfortably ensconced in his office in Montreal, he dreamed of an instant city of 50,000 people.

As one of his publicity brochures put it: "To this new port will come the ships of the Seven Seas, ships of the East laden with silk and rice will soon be riding at anchor in this splendid harbour, to sail away laden with lumber; ships for the West with Wares of the West; ships from the shores of far-off continents, trading through the new and picturesque port of Prince Rupert...."

Charles Melville Hays envisioned Prince Rupert as being an instant city of 50,000.

The survey party under J. H. Pillsbury rapidly cleared a space for a tool shed and tents, and then started constructing a wharf. They cleared a right-of-way and laid out a single street straight into the wilderness up from the dock site. A year later, about 150 people were settled on the Island and a few essential businesses had been established. The general public, however, could not buy land until the railway company was prepared to launch a great sale of lots.

Walter Wicks, who had grown up in a nearby cannery, was an early visitor to the townsite. This is how he described it: "Here before our eyes a seaport was in the making, soon to be recognized as an important outlet to this north country. The workers, speculators, small businessmen, tinhorns, pimps, and prostitutes were forming a melting pot of human conglomerate in a narrow one-street town. Restaurants, flop houses, hardware stores, cheap clapboard rooming houses, gambling dens, and brothels were all in business side by side with very little evidence of lawful authority.

"Because it was still a company-controlled town without franchise, saloons were prohibited, but the blind pigs — camouflaged places where illegal liquor was sold — took care of the thirsty. Fist fights were common and occasional knife slashing gave life a little excitement. Through this human mess I walked as a boy of fourteen, and as an old northern saying goes, 'I got my eyes peeled'."

The man whose dreams were behind all this flurry of activity, Charles Melville Hays, was a practical railwayman, born and raised in the great American tradition of transcontinental railway building. The 19th century of North America saw the creation of such great railway fortunes as that of the Vanderbilts in the east and completion of many lines. On May 10, 1869, the golden spike was driven into the Central Pacific Railroad at Promontory Point, Utah, linking the Central Pacific and the Union Pacific lines east and west, the first transcontinental railway system in North America.

The founders of the Central Pacific, (later the Southern Pacific), had overcome incredible difficulties to make huge fortunes for themselves. They were the "Big Four": Charles Crocker, Mark Hopkins, Collis Huntington and Leland Stanford, sometimes known also as the "Robber Barons." Farther north, Canadian-born James J. Hill, the "Empire-builder," drove the Great Northern Railway through the mountains into Tacoma, and carved out a vast fortune.

The Canadian Pacific Railway, perhaps the most astonishing of them all, reached tidewater at Port Moody near Vancouver, on Burrard Inlet on July 4, 1886, with the arrival of the first passenger train from Montreal. Construction of the C.P.R. had entailed incredible difficulties, crossing the vast empty central plains and over-

Prince Rupert is born — surveyors' wooden building and tents, May 1906. Rocks and muskeg of the area made building very difficult.

The dock in 1908. Although the railway tracks look impressive, full transcontinental service didn't begin until 1914.

coming the formidable barriers of the Rocky and Coast Mountains. The founders were rewarded with great wealth, peerages and knighthoods: Lord Mount Stephen, Lord Strathcona, Lord Shaughnessy and Sir William Van Horne. Charles Hays must have looked at their accomplishments with admiration and envy.

Not only was he a practical railwayman, he was a dreamer of dreams, with great powers of persuasion and personal drive. He was a promoter and an organizer, a financial genius. Some, however, might have called him a con man. He knew exactly what he wanted and he followed his dreams with determination and self confidence.

He believed that anything the Canadian Pacific could do, he could do better. He could build a transcontinental line across Canada on a shorter route and a better road bed. The C.P.R. had created a great western terminus at Vancouver. He would build his own terminus from bed rock at Prince Rupert. The C.P.R. had built the finest hotels in Canada. He would build better hotels. The C.P.R. built bridges and trestles of wood. He would build them of steel. The C.P.R. had built great ocean liners and coastal steamers. He would build better ships. All he needed was money and the opportunity and both were available.

The Grand Trunk Railway of Canada had been founded by British investors in 1852 to build a line between Montreal and Toronto. The next year it extended its rails from Montreal to Portland, Maine, making it a major force in pre-confederation transportation. It continued to extend its lines throughout Ontario and neighboring American territory, but its management became over-complacent. By the turn of the century the upstart C.P.R. was cutting deeply into its profits.

The London directors of the rather stodgy Grand Trunk decided that their company needed some of the American vigor that animated the C.P.R. As a result, in 1896 they hired Charles Melville Hays, a rising young American of 30, to become their general manager. He arrived on the scene like a breath of fresh air — although perhaps "small storm" would be a better description. Born at Rock Island, Illinois, he had already become general manager of the Wabash System when he arrived in Canada to revive the flagging fortunes of the old Grand Trunk. No detail escaped his eye.

Between 1896 and 1902 Hays turned a deficit of some $18 million into a profit of twice that, or some $36 million. His success gained the attention of the great Southern Pacific Railway in the United States, and for 18 months in 1901-1902 he was lured away to become president of that line. But early in 1902 he was back in Canada as general manager of the Grand Trunk, his ambition a great expansion westward. So great were his powers of persuasion and determination the London directors fell under his spell. He convinced them of the profits to be made from expansion into the vast unoccupied prairie lands of the West and the sale of town lots in new cities between Winnipeg and the Pacific Ocean. What the C.P.R. had done, he could do better, he emphasized.

They acted quickly. The Grand Trunk Pacific Railway, a subsidiary of the Grand Trunk, with Hays at the helm as general manager, was incorporated in 1903 to build a new Canadian transcontinental railway. He became company president two years later and the railway was on its way westward, starting on August 29, 1905. Years of feverish activity followed.

A new route had to be planned across the plains and through the mountains. Ships must be ordered to carry passengers and supplies on the Pacific to the new tidewater terminus, and river

In the early 1900s the two largest communities in the northern one-half of B.C. were Port Essington, above, at the mouth of the Skeena River and Hazelton, below, 180 miles up the canyon-studded waterway.

boats built to carry supplies through the awesome canyons of the Skeena River. As the result of a nation-wide contest, Hays chose the name Prince Rupert for his new city, after the cousin of King Charles II who in 1670 had been the first governor of the Hudson's Bay Company which had opened the Canadian plains to the fur traders.

The town of Prince Rupert was to have a special place in Hays' affections. Only he could have looked fondly on the bare rocks, the water-logged ground and the raw tree stumps that marked the townsite in 1906. In one of his publicity pamphlets that year he prophesied that Prince Rupert would become, "The most perfectly laid out and most beautiful city in the Dominion ... the Washington of Canada."

He might occasionally have pondered the old Greek proverb: "Those whom the gods wish to destroy, they first drive mad."

His engineers laid out a transcontinental route across the prairies, parallel in many areas to the C.P.R., but generally tapping the more fertile northern plains. The right-of-way ran through the Yellowhead Pass in the Rockies, a better grade than those taken by the C.P.R. through Kicking Horse Pass and Crowsnest Pass further south. It was one also taken by the competing Canadian Northern Pacific Railway. The rails followed the headwaters of the Fraser River from Tete Jaune Cache to Fort George (later to be called Prince George). Then they ran

The 180 miles of railway from Prince Rupert up the Skeena to Hazelton took nearly six years to build.

The photo below shows the first passenger train over the initial 100 miles on June 14, 1911.

up the Nechako River to its headwaters, across the divide to the fertile valley of the Bulkley River, down that stream to the Skeena River at Hazelton, and then through the gorges of the Skeena canyons to the new terminus of Prince Rupert. His route was 500 miles closer to the Orient than Vancouver.

The line between Prince Rupert and Hazelton took nearly six years to complete, with more than 1,200 surveys made through the dense mountains and swift rivers. The 184 miles of track has been described as "the most difficult section of railway ever to be built in North America." There were nearly two miles of tunnels in the Skeena section, while in the estuary section leading to the terminus, cribbing and heavy piling had to be installed, behind which dykes were built to dam sloughs and backwaters.

Despite the mountain barriers, the Grand Trunk Pacific's easy grade to the Pacific did not exceed four-tenths of one per cent at any point on the 4,000 miles of track from coast to coast. Maximum grade over the entire line is only 21 feet to the mile.

In addition to the rock and river and mountain barriers of nature, there was a formidable man-made barrier — money. Where did the vast amounts come from to undertake this huge construction project? Charles Melville Hays was as much a wizard at raising money as he was at creating a railroad. With his compulsive sales

On the Skeena River section, flat-bottomed sternwheel steamers were the workhorses during railway construction. Below are the Grand Trunk Pacific's vessels — *Omineca, Conveyor, Distributor,* and *Operator.* They successfully challenged some 180 miles of the canyon-studded Skeena River.

Although many communities sprang up along the railway, not all survived. One was Tete Jaune Cache on the Fraser River near Mt. Robson in the Rockies. The photo above shows its flooded main street in 1913. Next year the river washed the entire community down the Fraser River.

Another new community was South Fort George at the junction of the Fraser and Nechako Rivers in Central B.C. It also disappeared, absorbed by today's thriving city of Prince George.

technique, he persuaded conservative British financiers to open their purse strings. Equally as important, he convinced Prime Minister Laurier of the need for a railway line to compete with the C.P.R. monopoly. He secured huge land grants, including Kaien Island, and an astonishing government guarantee of 75 per cent of the company's bond issues. No other salesman could have been more convincing. He and Prime Minister Sir Wilfrid Laurier became close friends, a great help in times of crisis.

Every facet of the construction required miracles of organization. Contractors for the far western division were Foley, Welch and Stewart. They were faced with the greatest problems of anywhere on the line, particularly through the Skeena River gorges. Here construction camps were built every two miles. There had long been sternwheel boats plying the river as far up as Hazelton, but the Grant Trunk early recognized the need to run their own boats to get the supplies and work forces up to the numerous construction camps.

First of the new river boats was the *Distributor*, built at Victoria in the spring of 1908 by Alex Watson Jr., long an expert in the construction of sternwheelers. In her first season on the river she was chartered by the Hudson's Bay Company to deliver supplies to their trading post at Hazelton. Her first skipper was a veteran of the river, Captain Stewart Johnson, borrowed from the Hudson's Bay Company.

So successful was the *Distributor* that three similar vessels, all purely freight boats, were ordered at Victoria by the G.T.P. The *Conveyor* was completed in late 1908, followed by the *Operator* in 1909. The fourth vessel was laid down as the *Contractor*, but was completed as the *Omineca* for Foley, Welch and Stewart, who also took over the other ships, using steamboat captains from the Yukon.

"All of these Yukon captains thought they were pretty good men on the Yukon River," wrote Skeena pioneer Wiggs O'Neill, "but when they hit the old Skeena, all had a lot to learn. They said the Skeena was a bearcat compared to what they were used to. The captains of the Skeena all knew the river like a book and had become used to all the bends and turns and white water. However, it didn't take those men from the Yukon long to catch up."

The three original G.T.P. vessels had subsequent unusual careers. Their work on the Skeena was finished by 1911, so the machinery and fittings of the *Distributor* were taken overland to Kamloops and installed in a new *Distributor*. It worked on railway construction on the North Thompson River for the Canadian Northern Pacific Railway, which was building the rival transcontinental line to the G.T.P. After that railway was completed the hull was converted to a barge, and the machinery and fittings were shipped to the Mackenzie River. Here they were again built into a new hull for the Hudson's Bay Company as *Distributor III*. She had a long career as a passenger carrier and freighter on that river, and even appeared on a Canadian postage stamp.

Conveyor was refitted in similar fashion in 1912 at Tete Jaune Cache at the upper reaches of the Fraser after her sections had been taken overland to Edmonton and then through the Yellowhead Pass via the newly completed section of the G.T.P. She worked for Foley, Welch and Stewart on the Upper Fraser during G.T.P. construction, and occasionally between South Fort George and Soda Creek during the work on the Pacific Great Eastern (now British Columbia Railway). She was beached in 1915 and broken up four years later. *Operator* had a similar career between Tete Jaune Cache and Fort George from 1912 to 1915.

CHAPTER TWO

The *Prince Rupert* in her Grand Trunk colors. She was to sail for over 50 years.

The Prince Ships

Establishment of a first-class passenger service on the Pacific Coast to the new port of Prince Rupert was high on Hays' agenda, and he wanted only the best. In the first quarter of the century the Princess liners of the C.P.R.'s B.C. coast steamship service were considered among the finest short seas vessels in the world. They provided superb service to the coast waters of British Columbia, Puget Sound and the Alaska panhandle. Hays decided to call his new ships Princes and to run them in competition with the C.P.R. on several comparable routes.

In the early days of Grand Trunk Pacific construction many tons of supplies had to be freighted from Vancouver to Prince Rupert and three Scottish sea captains quickly took advantage of the opportunity. Captains Simon, Duncan and William Mackenzie were owners of Mackenzie Brothers Steamship Company Ltd. which operated small flat-bottomed freighters on the Lower Fraser River, and an ancient tug and barge. They contracted with the Grand Trunk to provide a regular freight and passenger service between Vancouver and Prince Rupert. As a result, they acquired a miscellaneous fleet. Their passenger ship, the *Powhatan*, was taken on bare-boat charter in 1908 from the British shipowners, Watts, Watts and Company, Ltd., and was appropriately renamed *Rupert City*.

She had been built at Barrow, England, for the Mediterranean and New York Steamship Company of Liverpool in 1886. With a gross tonnage of 2,536 and net tonnage of 1,640, her length at the waterline was 310.3 feet, beam 38.1 feet, and depth 25.2 feet. Her single screw drove a four-cylinder triple expansion engine of 1,400 i.h.p., giving a service speed of 11 knots. Before her arrival in British Columbia waters she had been employed by Watts, Watts in transporting Chinese laborers between Hong Kong and the west coast of Mexico during railway construction there.

She arrived at Vancouver on December 7, 1908, and was quickly given improved passenger accommodation in a False Creek shipyard. The after well deck was fitted with staterooms, and a dining saloon seating 125 was installed. More cabins were placed in the superstructure which was built on the promenade deck and extended to the forward end of the short poop deck. She carried eight lifeboats.

When the work was completed *Rupert City* advertised space for 160 first-class passengers and 250 in steerage. On one voyage she carried a record number of 500 construction workers for the railway. She was advertised to sail every Sunday from Seattle and Vancouver to Prince Rupert under command of Captain Duncan Mackenzie. Her first departure from Seattle was on May 30, 1909.

She soon made the headlines. On August 27, 1909, she went to the aid of the Alaska Steamship Company's liner *Ohio* which had struck a rock off Steep Point in Finlayson Channel. Some of the shipwrecked passengers were delivered to Vancouver.

With the arrival of the new *Prince Rupert* and *Prince George* on the west coast in 1909, *Rupert City* became redundant and was laid up in Vancouver. After a few trips to Australia with

lumber she was sold at auction in Seattle to Dodwell and Company who sailed her from Tacoma to Yokohama on October 13, 1913. She was then sold to Japanese owners, and renamed *Chinto Maru*. On January 4, 1917, during World War One she was torpedoed and sunk off the southwestern coast of Spain.

In 1903 Mackenzie Brothers had picked up at a bargain price the old iron barque *Henriette*, built in France in 1874, which had run ashore in 1901 on the Columbia River bar. Her new owners installed twin screws and primitive passenger accommodation. She was 160 feet long by 30 feet beam and 18.9 feet depth, and was powered by two, 16 h.p. engines. She was grossly underpowered. It was said that in any kind of head wind she went backwards instead of forwards, although her engines were full speed ahead. Under the best conditions, her progress was erratic, to say the least.

The other vessels in the Mackenzie fleet were the 95-foot tug *Escort No. 2*, built in Oregon in 1882, and the car barge *Georgian*, formerly owned by the Esquimalt and Nanaimo Railway. There was no lack of freight offering from the Grand Trunk. C. M. Hays was a railwayman, not a shipping man, so he came to depend greatly on the advice of the canny Scotsmen. He recommended that the railway company follow closely the successful formula used by Captain J. W. Troup in creating the C.P.R.'s Princess fleet, of which the two largest vessels were the *Princess Victoria* of 1903 and *Princess Charlotte* of 1908. The *Victoria* ran on the triangle route between Victoria, Vancouver and Seattle. The *Charlotte* was destined for a long successful career on both the southern and northern coast routes, and later as a cruise ship in the Mediterranean where 56 years later she ended her career under Greek ownership in 1964.

In May 1909 the *Rupert City* became the first vessel to carry passengers to Prince Rupert.

MACKENZIE BROS. STEAMSHIP COMPANY, Limited

Operating Passenger and Freight Steamers between Vancouver, Northern British Columbia, and Southeast Alaska

Only Direct Service between Vancouver and Prince Rupert

3,000 tons register, 6 water-tight compartments, double bottom, practically unsinkable.

Every [modern convenience including
WIRELESS TELEGRAPH SYSTEM

Classed A1 at Lloyds

SS. "RUPERT CITY"

D. MACKENZIE, MASTER

Accommodation for 250 First-Class Passengers, 250 Steerage Passengers

Leaves Vancouver for Prince Rupert - - - - Every Monday

Leaves Prince Rupert for Vancouver - - - - Every Thursday

FARES - - - First Class **$15.** Steerage **$6.00**

It was very rare at that time for coastwise ships to flaunt three funnels, but Captain Troup had so specified when he ordered his two record-breakers. Hays decided that the two new Grand Trunk ships should copy their rivals in this respect and that they should operate on similar routes. They would be named after royal princes rather than princesses, and were expected to outclass their competition in speed. He even went to the same English shipbuilders who had built the *Princess Victoria,* Swan, Hunter and Wigham Richardson Ltd., of Newcastle-on-Tyne.

The two new ships were named *Prince Rupert* and *Prince George* and designed by an eminent naval architect, Richard Lane Newman. As an example of progressive thinking in ship design, they were the first passenger liners to be built with cruiser sterns. *Prince Rupert* was launched on December 13, 1909, nearly three months before her sister, and ran her sea trials early in 1910. To prepare for her arrival, the Grand Trunk Pacific built new wharves at Vancouver, Victoria, Seattle and Prince Rupert.

Identical in appearance, each was 3,379 gross tons and 1,626 net, and had two overall decks — a bridge deck plated in amidships and a long boat deck. There was a full length double bottom and a total water ballast of 606 tons. Only 350 tons of cargo could be carried. On an overall length of 320 feet, the registered dimensions were 306.7 feet between perpendiculars, 42.2 feet in breadth and 23.9 depth. Draft was 15 feet 7 inches.

Main engines were four-cylinder, triple-expansion sets with cylinders 23½, 37, 41 and 41 inches in diameter and stroke of 33 inches developing 6,500 i.h.p. at full speed. Two double-ended and two single-ended boilers worked 180 pounds per square inch under forced draft. They burned coal originally, but in 1912 were con-

The *Prince George* at Prince Rupert. She brought Prime Minister Laurier to the new community.

verted to oil fuel. Maximum service speed was 19 knots.

Accommodation was provided for 200 first-class passengers and 36 second class. On excursions, 1,500 passengers could be carried. They were six feet longer and two feet wider in beam than the rival *Princess Victoria*, but a little smaller than *Princess Charlotte*. They were smart, racy looking vessels with three very tall, slim funnels. Originally they had pale grey hulls, white bridge decks and superstructure and black funnels, each with a broad white band, of which the centre one carried the G.T.P. monogram. Both were originally registered at Newcastle-on-Tyne, but subsequently at Prince Rupert. Later, their hulls were painted black and the funnels became all black, the centre one only being adorned with a green maple leaf in a red circle, accompanied by the letters G.T.P.

Prince Rupert, on arrival on the Pacific coast, was placed under the command of Captain B.L. "Barney" Johnson, who had formerly commanded ships of the Union Steamship Company of B.C. Ltd., and the Boscowitz Steamship Company on the coast. He was to have a long and notable career as shipmaster, pilot, submarine commander, naval officer in both World War One and Two, shipowner and businessman.

The new ship met with a rapturous reception. The *Seattle Times* of June 11, 1910, reported: "With her hull and bulwarks gleaming like ivory in the fitful sunshine, the new Grand Trunk Pacific liner *Prince Rupert*, from Newcastle-on-Tyne, drew into her slip at the foot of Madison Street this morning while vessels in the harbour shrieked a true Seattle welcome to the officers and men aboard."

Prince George, her sister ship, arrived a month later. She was placed under the command of Captain G. E. L. Robertson, who had been chief officer of the *Rupert*. The two ships were identical and few could tell them apart. One difference, so it was said, was that the officers and the crew of the *Rupert* spoke English, while those on the *George* spoke Gaelic — a legacy of the Mackenzie brothers, who recruited Gaelic speakers from the western isles of Scotland. General superintendent of the Grand Trunk shipping operations was Captain Charles H. Nicholson.

Soon after her arrival, *Prince George* carried an important passenger. In August she took Prime Minister Laurier and his entourage from Vancouver to have a first-hand look at the new terminal port of Prince Rupert. The Prime Minister took the opportunity to make an announcement that the government would subsidize construction of a new drydock and shipyard there capable of handling ships of 20,000 tons — another result of Hays' salesmanship. It was completed in 1916.

Prince Rupert, however, was not the first Grand Trunk Pacific ship to show her colors on the coast. In November 1909 the company received the Dominion government contract for $200 a trip to provide mail and passenger service from Vancouver and Prince Rupert to the Queen Charlotte Islands, previously provided by the C.P.R. steamer *Amur*. The Islands had long been neglected by governments and had only a scant population, dependent upon mining, logging and fishing. During the heady boom days of 1910 and 1911 there were hopes for a prosperous future for the Islands, and settlers began to pour in, attracted by colorful real estate advertisements.

To meet the demands of the new contract, the Grand Trunk Pacific Coast Steamship Company was incorporated on May 26, 1910, and the little steamer *Prince Albert* succeeded the plodding *Henriette* on the Vancouver, Prince Rupert and Queen Charlotte run. She was purchased sec-

Captain B. L. Johnson on the *Prince Rupert's* bridge with C. M. Hays, center, and Sir Waldron Smithers who is commemorated by the community of Smithers.

The *Prince Rupert* arriving at her home port on June 15, 1910.

The *Prince Rupert*, below, cruising Alaska's Inside Passage before World War Two. This cruise gains in popularity every year, with some 300,000 passengers a season visiting the mountains and glaciers in majestic vessels of 70,000 tons and more —— 20 times the size of the pioneer vessels on the route. Fares, though, are considerably higher than the one quoted in the opposite advertisement.

The *Prince Albert* when she arrived at Masset on June 23, 1910, to a royal welcome.

ond-hand in England where she had been built in 1892 as the *Bruno* for Thomas Wilson's Sons and Company Ltd. They had operated her on a freight and passenger service between Hull and Antwerp. Her dimensions were 232 feet by 30 feet by 14.1 feet. She provided little in the way of luxury, but was certainly an improvement over her predecessor. Soon Captain Simon Mackenzie went to find a better ship.

The *Henriette*, operated under charter by the G.T.P. in 1909, was purchased in 1910, and put on freighting as soon as *Prince Albert* arrived. The latter made her initial trip to Masset on June 23, 1910, and was given a royal welcome with speeches and banners flying. She was commanded by Captain Cecil Wearmouth.

Another addition was the new coastwise freighter *Amethyst* purchased in Scotland by Captain Simon Mackenzie. She had been completed by Scott and Sons of Greenock for prominent Glasgow shipowner William Robertson, owner of the Gem Line.

She was a remarkably well-built vessel, designed for freighting around the stormy seas of the British Isles. The ship was 185.3 feet long, 29.6 feet beam and 13.3 feet in moulded depth. Her triple expansion engines gave her a speed of 12 knots. Mackenzie personally designed and supervised the work which converted the *Amethyst* into the very efficient little passenger ship *Prince John*, with accommodation for 44 first-class passengers, all with berths. She sailed from Glasgow on May 16, 1911, arriving at Victoria on July 11. Captain Wearmouth then took command and Captain Duncan Mackenzie of the *Escort No. 2* took over the *Prince Albert*.

The *Prince Rupert* on the rocks at Genn Island.

CHAPTER THREE

Good Luck and Hard Luck Ships

Prince Albert continued an undistinguished career until August 18, 1914, when she came close to disaster. She ran up high and dry on Butterworth Rocks, off Melville Island, not far from Prince Rupert. She appeared to be beyond salvage, but was eventually refloated, repaired, and lead an adventurous life for another 35 years.

The little *Prince John* had a long and faithful career on the Queen Charlotte Islands run and quickly won the affection of the Islanders. Crossing the shallow Hecate Strait from Prince Rupert was often very unpleasant, but she was a wonderful sea boat, even in the worst of weather. An old-timer wrote of her affectionately in 1930: "To the scattered people of the Islands, the *John* is more than a ship. She is an institution, a parent and a friend. Often they swear at her; more often they swear by her. She is as steady and as perenially welcome as the rising sun. She crawls into holes with her belly barely clear of the mangling rocks. She pounds for days into southeast seas, with chairs charging adrift in her dining room, all to bring mail and provisions and the grace of contact with the outside world to a score of lonely camps and settlements."

She had her share of accidents, but the most serious occurred on March 30, 1920, when *Prince Albert* collided with her off Dead Tree Point near Skidegate Inlet. The *Prince John*, under Captain W. W. Moorhouse, left Queen Charlotte City at 5:45 a.m. bound for Prince Rupert. The weather was fine with occasional snow squalls, the wind fresh off the land. The *Albert* had left Prince Rupert the night before under Captain H. L. Robertson. At 6:35 a.m. *Prince John* was overtaken by a heavy snowstorm which obliterated all aids of navigation. Captain Moorhouse determined to turn about. Almost at the same moment, the *Albert* loomed out of the snow, close on the *John's* starboard bow.

She hit *Prince John* 24 feet from the stern. If it had been amidships the ship might have sunk in a few moments. To keep the hole in the *Prince John* plugged, Captain Robertson ordered full speed ahead, but it took an hour and a half to beach the sinking ship in shallow water. All the *John's* passengers and crew scrambled aboard the *Albert* and mail and valuables were saved. *Prince John* sank to upper deck level but was subsequently raised by the salvage vessel *Algerine*. In the court of enquiry both captains were exonerated from blame and commended for their resourcefulness and coolness.

Meanwhile, *Prince Rupert* and *Prince George* had proved very successful and popular ships on the express service between Vancouver and Prince Rupert and the triangle run between Vancouver, Victoria and Seattle, which necessitated an average speed of 16.8 knots. *Prince Rupert* would leave Prince Rupert at 9 a.m. on a Monday, and arrive at Vancouver at 4:30 p.m. Tuesday; sail at 6 p.m. for Victoria, arriving at 10:30 p.m. and sailing at midnight to Seattle, arriving at 6 a.m. On Wednesday she sailed at 9 a.m. for Victoria, arriving at 1:30 p.m., and leaving at 4 p.m. for Vancouver, arriving at 8:30 p.m. Then at midnight she sailed for Prince Rupert,

Above: The *Prince Albert* wrecked on Butterworth Rocks in 1914. She was salvaged and continued to serve under various owners. She was finally converted to a log barge and foundered off Vancouver Island in 1950.

Below: The *Prince John* ashore near Skidegate. She was also salvaged and in 1940 sold to the Union Steamship Company. As the *Cassiar* she served another 11 years, in all plying B.C.'s coastal waters for four decades.

making 17.5 knots, arriving at 9 a.m. Friday and sailing at 9 a.m. the next day for the south. Thus each ship made a complete round trip every five days and had only one clear day layover. It was an arduous schedule requiring great care by the crew while navigating the tortuous Inside Passage.

In later years, with the development of pulp mills and mining camps, such as Ocean Falls, Swanson Bay, Surf Inlet, Anyox and Stewart, the schedules were modified to suit the changing conditions. Service to Seattle was badly disrupted in August 1914 when the new G.T.P. docks burned at a loss of $400,000. The triangle service was discontinued in March 1923, not to be resumed until 1930, and then only briefly.

During their long careers on the British Columbia coast, *Prince Rupert* was considered an unlucky ship and *Prince George* a lucky one, although she had an unlucky end.

The first serious accident to the *Rupert* occurred on March 23, 1917, when she ran ashore on Genn Island, shortly after leaving Prince Rupert for Anyox. In a 70-mile-an-hour gale, and in poor visibility, Captain Duncan Mackenzie ran his ship onto a rocky beach where she rested on an even keel only 30 feet from the adjacent forest. Passengers were able to walk ashore and there were no casualties. Pinnacles of rock had to be blasted away before the ship could be refloated and towed into Prince Rupert drydock for repairs.

Some two years later she was the victim of an extraordinary accident while lying at her berth in Vancouver on January 14, 1919, waiting to sail north. She was struck by lightning which fractured her after mast about a foot from the truck and forced her to proceed to Victoria ahead of time for her annual refit.

Her next accident occurred in the following October when fire was found in her cargo hold while she was outward bound from Vancouver. She was forced to return to port while the damage was repaired at a cost of $25,000.

The most serious accident of her career occurred on September 20, 1920, when she struck a reef while entering the pulp mill port of Swanson Bay, near Princess Royal Island, in heavy fog. Her master showed great coolness and skill in running his vessel on the beach, thus effecting a safe landing for passengers and crew without mishap. There was a 12-foot tear in the ship's bottom and at high tide she was completely submerged, with the exception of a portion of the bridge and upper deck.

Pacific Salvage Company of Victoria sent their salvage vessel *Algerine* to the scene. The first difficulty was to get the ship on an even keel, for her stern was in 72 feet of water and the bow in 20 feet only. Just the tips of her three funnels were visible. This part of the job was accomplished by the use of two 1,400 ton barges. A cofferdam was then built on the ship, not around it. In other words, the sides of the ship were built up to such an extent as to place them below the water level at low tide. This task entailed several weeks of work and the building of a structure 75 feet high, 175 feet long and 42 feet broad above the shade deck. The uprights of this cofferdam were bolted to the ship's sides and planked up on the outside, with all cracks and crevices covered with heavy canvas.

More than 125,000 feet of lumber was used in the cofferdam which, with the enormous weight of the canvas, iron fastenings and other attachments added nearly 200 tons of additional weight to the ship. Then a battery of six-inch and twelve-inch pumps was used to raise the ship to the surface. She was towed to Victoria, and after substantial repairs by Yarrows Ltd. was able to return to service.

The next serious accident to *Prince Rupert*

The *Prince Rupert* after striking a reef at Swanson Bay. At high tide, below, she was virtually submerged, her stern in 72 feet of water. Beside her is the salvage vessel *Algerine*.

The massive cofferdam built to raise the *Prince Rupert* was 75 feet high and weighed 200 tons.

happened in the early morning hours of August 22, 1927, when she was southbound to Vancouver from Prince Rupert with a full passenger list. Shortly after 6 a.m., in poor visibility and with a strong ebb tide running in Seymour Narrows, she struck the notorious Ripple Rock head on and passed clear over it. She stopped her engines, but the strength of the ebb tide forced her astern so that she struck a second time. She pinned herself on the rock, completely immobilized, with one of her propellers in mid-air. In addition, her rudder had been driven into, and interlocked with the starboard propeller. Her position was extremely hazardous for she was very close to the cliff on the starboard side of the narrow channel.

Fortunately, S.S. *Cardena* of the Union Steamship Company was not far away and heard *Prince Rupert's* distress signals. Captain Andy Johnson brought his ship into the dangerous current and made *Cardena* fast alongside *Prince Rupert's* port side. With consummate seamanship he managed to get a steel towing line on to the stern and pulled the vessel off the sharp pinnacle.

"First we got her into mid-channel and safe from the threatening cliffs," Captain Johnson reported, "thus preventing a major disaster. Then we towed her back to a safe anchorage in Deep Cove, just a mile from the Narrows entrance, towing being difficult owing to the *Rupert's* rudder being jammed hard a-starboard."

In Deep Cove, Captain Johnson transferred as many passengers as he could accommodate aboard *Cardena*, with all the cargo, mail and express. The passing C.P.R. steamer *Princess Beatrice* picked up the remainder of the passengers and two tugs towed the stricken *Prince Rupert* to Burrard Dry Dock in Vancouver. The speedy action of *Cardena* saved the *Rupert* from almost certain disaster. The Union Steamship

Company, in an extremely friendly gesture, waived all salvage claims.

For many years, Ripple Rock, in the center of swift-running Seymour Narrows near the city of Campbell River, was the most dangerous menace to navigation in the Inside Passage between Vancouver and Prince Rupert. Scores of ships, large and small, struck the rock. Over the years several unsuccessful attempts were made to remove it. During one drilling operation in 1945 nine men in a work boat were drowned when it overturned in the raging current.

Another demolition was undertaken by the Dominion Government in 1957-58. A shaft over 500 feet deep was drilled on nearby Maud Island, from which a tunnel was pushed through solid granite to the base of Ripple Rock. A shaft was then bored up to the surface. Around the twin peaks of the rock a hole was excavated and filled with a powerful new blasting agent.

April 5, 1958, was the date for the great explosion. I was hiding with a photographer in a safe bunker on the shore north of Campbell River and watched the spectacular blast, which was a complete success. Ripple Rock was no more, destroyed in what was claimed to be the biggest non-nuclear explosion up to that date.

At the time of the Ripple Rock accident, *Prince Rupert* was under command of Captain Dan Donald, also in charge when she met her next serious mishap on March 6, 1931. It happened when she lay alongside the Yarrows Ltd. dock at Esquimalt where she was undergoing annual overhaul. Shortly before midnight watchmen noticed water running into the hold. The alarm was given. So quickly did the ship fill, however, that crew members, aroused from sleep, only had time to escape in the clothing that they picked up as they hastily quit their quarters.

The ship soon keeled over with a list of 45°

until her stern lay on the bottom in 26 feet of water. To prevent her from keeling over farther on her side, ropes were placed around her masts and fastened to the shore. It was subsequently ascertained that the crew had been painting a compartment close to the waterline and left a porthole open to help the drying process. With a rising tide, water began to flow through the porthole. It was too late to stop the inrush, and for the second time in her career *Prince Rupert* lay on her side.

Fortunately, the salvage steamer *Salvage King* was lying alongside the same dock, and with her powerful pumps and the assistance of the salvage tug *Respond*, the stricken vessel was brought upright. It had taken her about an hour to keel over from the time the inrush of water was first noticed. Forty members of the crew scrambled for safety, and only one man was injured from falling down a companionway. It took about a month before the ship was ready for sea again.

Another serious accident to *Prince Rupert* occurred in the early morning hours of August 30, 1951, when she was northbound to Ketchikan from Prince Rupert at a reduced speed of 10 knots because of heavy fog. *Princess Kathleen*, crack cruise liner of the Canadian Pacific fleet, was southbound from Ketchikan with 294 passengers. At 4:33 a.m. *Prince Rupert* suddenly appeared out of the fog and crashed into the *Kathleen's* port bow. She caused heavy damage, but fortunately nobody was injured. The ships were then off Lord Rock, 32 miles north of Prince Rupert. The *Rupert*, under command of Captain W. E. Eccles, cut half way through the main deck of the *Kathleen*, making a V-shaped, 28-foot gap close to the waterline.

The second officer was in charge on the bridge of *Prince Rupert*. At about 4:25 a.m. radar bearings had confirmed the presence of

The *Prince Rupert* in wartime colors aground just inside Prince Rupert Harbour in 1942. As in previous groundings, she was successfully refloated. Four years later in Ketchikan, Alaska, however, the first *Prince George* wasn't so fortunate. She caught fire and was destroyed.

the C.P.R. steamer about two and a half miles distant and nine degrees off the starboard bow. The officer of the watch sounded fog signals, giving two short blasts to indicate his helm movements and put the engines at stand-by. He then altered course five degrees to port and later a further five degrees to port. At 4:30 he heard several long blasts from the *Kathleen*, about four degrees off the starboard bow. He put his vessel hard-a-port and ordered the engines full astern but it was too late. The crash was inevitable.

The damage was extensive. Repairs to the *Kathleen* were estimated at $250,000, while the *Rupert's* damage was estimated at $100,000. Both ships were found to blame and the certificates of the two second officers on watch were suspended for three months.

The career of *Prince George* was generally luckier than that of her sister. She had a few troubles soon after her arrival from England. On one occasion she ran high and dry in the First Narrows, at the entrance to Vancouver harbour, but was soon refloated without serious damage.

She had a serious collision on October 14, 1912, in Puget Sound when the small halibut steamer *Lief E.*, loaded with 30,000 pounds of fish, struck her in heavy fog. Captain Duncan Mackenzie of *Prince George* lowered boats to pick up the eight-man crew of the auxiliary schooner. With fine seamanship he passed steel cables under the sinking vessel and towed her to Harbor Island, Seattle, where she was beached.

On July 23, 1920, she struck the North Bluff in Seymour Narrows but was able to continue to Prince Rupert for drydocking. On December 30, 1933, she stranded for a short time on Vadso Rock, near Anyox, and on December 20, 1937, she ran ashore for a short time off Kingcome Point, Princess Royal Island, in a snowstorm.

Her end came on September 22, 1945, at Ketchikan when a fuel tank exploded, killing one man in the engine room, and setting the ship ablaze. Captain Neil MacLean, a veteran of the company since 1910 who had long commanded *Prince John* on the Queen Charlotte Islands run, and was one of the Gaelic speakers, managed to beach the blazing ship on a rock in the harbour. In true maritime tradition, he remained aboard the smouldering vessel until all passengers and crew were safely ashore. Although he had been at sea from the age of 12, he had never learned to swim. After the gutted hulk was towed to Gravina Island by the U.S. Coast Guard and beached to prevent the fire from spreading to the waterfront, Captain MacLean was still aboard.

A tug came along to get him off the beached vessel and told him to jump into the water. Not surprisingly, the doughty captain refused. As a consequence, the tug came right up to the still-blazing ship and he stepped over the rail on to the rescue vessel. The gutted hull of *Prince George* was towed to Seattle in 1949 where it was cut up for scrap.

CHAPTER FOUR

The Gumboot City

With the arrival of regular passenger service to Prince Rupert, the population grew to 3,000 by 1909. Conditions were still primitive and, above all, muddy. Citizens wore gumboots as a matter of course, and used an intricate system of boardwalks to avoid being mired in the ooze. But to Hays the streets were lined with gold, and his optimism never wavered.

He lured Francis Rattenbury, the eminent architect who had designed the provincial Parliament Buildings and the Empress Hotel at Victoria, away from the C.P.R. His instructions were to plan a string of resort hotels in the Rocky Mountains to capitalize on the scenery, then to provide Prince Rupert with civilized hotel accommodation. The Grand Trunk Pacific Inn was only a temporary wooden building which would have to make do until it could be replaced by a splendid new structure, worthy of a great seaport.

As designed by Rattenbury, the projected

Prince Rupert's waterfront about 1910. The large frame building is the Grand Trunk's Pacific Inn —— the "temporary" hotel which stood for over 50 years.

Rattenbury's sketch of the planned Prince Rupert transportation complex. The chateau was to be over twice as tall as Victoria's Empress Hotel, opposite, nearing completion. The Empress opened in 1908 and, greatly enlarged, still serves the public — a venerable Victoria landmark.

450-bedroom Chateau Prince Rupert would be worthy of Charles Hays' dreams, part of a great transportation complex. At the water's edge would be a long covered dock dominated by two, 60-foot-high cupola-topped towers. Passengers disembarking from a G.T.P. steamer would be enveloped in luxury the moment they stepped ashore. Just behind the steamship terminal, where the railway tracks hugged the shore, would be a deluxe station carefully designed to impress passengers alighting from G.T.P. trains with its splendor. And whether tourists arrived by boat or train, they would find themselves at the doorstep of the most imposing chateau-style hotel ever designed for the West.

Located on a slight rise above the steamship terminal and railway station, with its 450 bedrooms and its dining room capable of seating 265, it was expected to cost as much as $2 million. Twice as tall as the Empress Hotel in Victoria, it would reign over a garden city of formal parks, wide tree-lined boulevards and gently curving residential by-ways.

Such was the dream of Charles Melville Hays, as envisaged by Francis Rattenbury and New York's finest landscape artists. Alas, the dreams were to be shattered by an iceberg in the Atlantic.

Prince Rupert town lots were first put on sale in May 1909, even before the city was incorporated on March 3, 1910. To handle the exclusive campaign Hays incorporated the Grand Trunk Pacific Development Company Ltd., with his brother, David Hays, in charge. So convincing was the Hays publicity campaign that when the first town lots were auctioned at Vancouver's cavernous Denman Street arena, very spirited bidding from 1,500 eager purchasers pushed prices up to $8,000 for a single lot. In Prince Rupert itself, where purchasers could see what they were buying, the prices ranged from $50 to $6,000 per lot. Even in a sea of mud, boom prices prevailed.

Streets had to be built on trestles or blasted through rock bluffs. The rock work was staggering. Whole hillsides had to be levelled and then a further depth of rock removed to lay the sewers. The biggest cut of all was along the waterfront where 400,000 cubic yards of rock were removed to make the railway yards.

By 1910 the new city of Prince Rupert began to take shape, and the boom fuelled the optimism of Charles Melville Hays and the Grand Trunk directors. Track laying was going well and the London money market was firm. Hays laid plans for two new luxury hotels at Ottawa and Winnipeg. He was offered a knighthood by his friend, Sir Wilfrid Laurier, but declined it as it would have entailed surrender of his American citizenship.

Unfortunately, there were ominous shadows on the horizon. The economy was getting overheated, with two transcontinental railroads — the Grand Trunk Pacific and the Canadian Northern Pacific — competing for finance and manpower. Then in 1911 Sir Wilfrid Laurier and his Liberals lost power to a new Conservative government at Ottawa which was less bountiful in its largesse of land grants and subsidies. Worse, since the days of Sir John A. MacDonald, the Conservatives had always favored the C.P.R. With Laurier no longer at the helm, the future looked less bright for the Grand Trunk. In addition, some of the British financiers were getting restive as construction costs far exceeded the early estimates.

Charles Hays was not easily daunted. In the spring of 1912 he made a trip to London to explain his dreams for the future and raise more money. The Panama Canal was then under construction, and he argued prairie grain could be shipped out of Prince Rupert to Liverpool cheaper than via the Great Lakes. A grain elevator would have to be built. There were great resources of coal in the Peace River district of British Columbia and Alberta. All that was needed was British capital to develop and exploit these resources, shipping coal to world markets through a new facility at Prince Rupert. He expounded the great prospects of the port as a world fishing capital and persuaded British investors to establish the Canadian Fish and Cold Storage Company plant, later touted as the largest cold storage plant in the world.

After a round of whirlwind pep talks in London, Hays was anxious to get back to Canada for the gala opening of his grand new hotel at Ottawa, to be named after his good friend, Sir Wilfrid. He gladly accepted an offer from J. Bruce Ismay, chairman of the White Star Line, to be his personal guest on the maiden voyage to New York of the *Titanic*, largest ocean liner in the world.

Hays was accompanied by his wife, his daughter Margaret, their ladies' maid, his son-in-law Thornton Davidson, and his male private secretary, Vivian Payne. They had a deluxe suite on the promenade deck.

Tragedy struck at 11:40 p.m. on the night of April 14, 1912, when the "unsinkable" *Titanic* collided with an iceberg in the north Atlantic. The glancing blow ripped open the side of the ship. Charles Hays saw the ladies of his party safely into a lifeboat. He, his son-in-law, secretary and over 1,000 others went down with the ship. With him went his grandiose dreams, for it was said that "He carried his plans in his hip pocket." Sir Wilfrid Laurier had described him in 1911 as, "Beyond question the greatest railroad genius in Canada."

Today the name of Charles Melville Hays is almost forgotten. There is a railway divisional point in Saskatchewan called Melville. Hay-

The townsite in 1908, above, was a frontier community of stumps, tents and rough frame buildings. Because of the mud and muskeg, streets and sidewalks were built of planks. Centre Street, below, is typical.

By 1910, in Prince Rupert permanent buildings were replacing the tents and shacks of 1908. But when the first transcontinental train arrived on April 9, 1914, both Hays and the G.T.P. were dead — and so was the vision of a city of 50,000. But the community survived and is today an important northern B.C. city.

sport is a flag station at the mouth of the Skeena River, 24 miles southeast of Prince Rupert. Mount Hays is a modest hill of 2,322 feet on Kaien Island, and there is a statue of him in front of Prince Rupert's City Hall.

His body was recovered from the Atlantic and is buried in Montreal. The grand opening of the Chateau Laurier never took place. Instead there was a memorial service in the American Presbyterian Church.

J. Bruce Ismay survived in the last lifeboat to leave the *Titanic*. His career ruined, he had to face the verbal abuse and condemnation of the world. Perhaps Charles M. Hays was more fortunate. He did not live to see his dreams in ruins, the Grand Trunk Pacific Railway a financial disaster.

Unlike many first class passengers who survived the *Titanic*, Mrs. Hays did not sue the White Star Line, for she pointed out that she and her family had been guests of the company.

The Grand Trunk Pacific was far from completed when Hays died. Not until April 5, 1914, was the last spike driven at Fort Fraser in Central B.C. by his successor as president, Edson J. Chamberlin. Regular rail passenger service to Prince Rupert was inaugurated on September 6, 1914. But it was too late. War had been declared in Europe and the financial markets closed. By the fall of 1915 the G.T.P. was beginning to feel the pinch of World War One. The company was unable to pay the interest on its enormous debts, or meet its obligations to the Canadian government.

The end came on March 7, 1916, when the company was forced into receivership by the Canadian government. The disaster not only cost British investors huge sums of money but also left a long trail of resentment in Great Britain and suspicion of investment in Canada.

By then World War One had been raging for 18 bloody months with hundreds of thousands of soldiers already dead. Canada was deeply involved. When war broke out in August, 1914, there was panic in Victoria and Ottawa at the state of unpreparedness on the Pacific coast. The only naval protection was the obsolete light cruiser HMCS *Rainbow* at Esquimalt, while the powerful German cruisers *Leipzig* and *Nurnberg* were thought to be off the coast of Mexico. In fact, the *Leipzig* was being coaled at Mazatlan by the Vancouver coastal freighter *Cetriana* on July 31.

Rainbow was ordered to prepare for action, although she had no high-explosive ammunition. Lloyd's of London warned all shipping that both the German cruisers were operating on the west coast of North America. The directors of the Grand Trunk Pacific briefly ordered *Prince Rupert* and *Prince George* to seek safety in American waters. Rumors flew in rapid succession. *Rainbow* sailed for San Francisco, and was told by the British consul there that the German cruisers had been seen near San Diego, steering north. After leaving San Francisco the crew of *Rainbow* threw all inflammable woodwork overboard. When flotsam was found near the Golden Gate, the story quickly spread that the Canadian light cruiser had been sunk. In fact, her coal was running out and she headed north again.

In the state of panic that then prevailed at the Esquimalt naval base, it was decided to commandeer the Grand Trunk steamer *Prince George*, fit her out as a hospital ship, and send her to sea to look for survivors from *Rainbow*.

Command of the ship was given to Lieutenant-Commander A. M. Kinnersley Saul, R.N.R., who happened to be conveniently at hand as chief officer of the lighthouse tender *Quadra*. He was told that he was to have the entire Grand Trunk crew, 30 Royal Navy Canadian Volunteer Reserve seamen under a petty officer, and three

The *Prince George* as a hospital ship at anchor at Prince Rupert.

navy signalmen. The medical and nursing staff from the Royal Jubilee Hospital at Victoria were drafted and the city ransacked for medical supplies. Although *Prince George* was ready for action in four days, because of the wet weather it was impossible to paint her sides white with a green stripe, as required for hospital ships. Still with her black hull and three black funnels the ship crossed to Vancouver to paint the hull. A dry morning enabled the crew to paint only the port side white with the green stripe before the rain came down in torrents. The captain knew a red cross must be painted somewhere, so he placed it on the middle funnel. Only much later did he learn it should have been on the ship's side.

On the day that the crew painted the port side, *Prince George* learned that *Rainbow* had gone north in response to a report that an enemy cruiser had been seen in Queen Charlotte Sound. Presumably to look for survivors, the hospital ship sailed out of Vancouver harbour at full speed, painted white on one side and black on the other. It was a week before they got a sufficiently dry day to finish the paint job. Mean-

while, they encountered *Rainbow* which twice trained her guns on them under the impression that the sleek three-funnelled, cruiser-sterned steamer was a German cruiser. Afterwards in Prince Rupert, Commander Walter Hose of *Rainbow* told Lieutenant Commander Saul how near they were to being sunk. In fact, only the matron's white suede shoes drying at a porthole had saved them.

Meanwhile, in the town of Prince Rupert panic was so great that every ablebodied man was commandeered to shovel a stockpile of coal off the dock in case the enemy ships should come into port to refuel. *Prince George* had to go to Juneau, Alaska, for oil, but the American authorities only gave them enough to get back to Prince Rupert. A few weeks later she returned to Esquimalt, the only casualty having been a nurse's sprained ankle. After an admiral's inspection and congratulations on the efficiency of the ship, *Prince George* was decommissioned as a hospital ship and returned to civilian service. The German cruiser scare was over, so there was no need for her to seek sanctuary at Seattle.

CHAPTER FIVE

Strangled by Debt

If the war scare was over, financial troubles weren't. While the Grand Trunk Pacific Railway staggered under a load of debt and went into liquidation in March 1916, its great rival, the Canadian Northern Pacific Railway, ran into similar problems. It was the brainchild of two of the great railway promoters of the age, Mackenzie and Mann, (Sir William Mackenzie and Sir Donald Mann). Unlike their British and American rivals, they were native Canadians, born in rural Ontario. Mackenzie, a former school teacher, became the contractor for various local lines of the C.P.R. Donald Mann, burly and bearded, a former blacksmith, was the ideal partner for Mackenzie. They founded near the turn of the century the railway contracting firm of Mackenzie Mann and Company Ltd. In an era when railway builders had to be active in politics, Mackenzie was a Conservative and Mann a Liberal, so they were covered whichever party was in power.

They started their spectacular railway career in 1896 when they took up an option on the dormant Lake Manitoba Railway and Canal Company. This move gave them a government land grant and a bond issue guaranteed by the province of Manitoba. There were many such inactive or derelict little railway companies, and they took advantage of every bargain. Meanwhile, Mackenzie was building a fortune through his control of the Toronto street railway system and the money-making Brazilian Traction Company in South America.

Then in 1898 the partners became involved in the Klondike gold rush in the Yukon and promoted the Cassiar Central project, which was to

The *Prince Charles* with her clipper bow had the graceful lines of a millionaire's yacht.

be an all-Canadian route to the mines. This project entailed building a railway from Telegraph Creek on the Stikine River in northern British Columbia to connect with the Yukon River system at Teslin Lake. The project would have given them 700,000 acres of mineral-rich land.

A fleet of river boats was built by the C.P.R. to operate on the Stikine River, and they purchased two ocean liners, the *Tartar* and *Athenian*, to run from Vancouver to the river as part of the All-Canadian route. The first shipment of steel rails was actually unloaded on a bar at the

mouth of the Stikine when the entire project collapsed. Politics intervened, and the Canadian Senate killed the land subsidy bill. The steel rails rusted on what became known as Mackenzie and Mann Bar until they were removed for scrap during World War Two.

The partners were unperturbed. They incorporated the Canadian Northern Railway in 1899, and started an inexorable move westward across the prairies. During the next 20 years they created some 10,000 miles of transcontinental railway across Canada, parallel in many sections to the C.P.R. They opened up much rich farming land on the prairies and their ambitions seemed boundless. In the Rocky Mountains their line ran parallel to the Grand Trunk Pacific through the Yellowhead Pass, down the North Thompson River to Kamloops, and then parallel to the C.P.R. via the Fraser River canyon to a terminus they called Port Mann near New Westminster.

The project was irrational and a great waste of money, but in those years of railway building madness, governments and private investors poured countless millions into the Canadian Northern. William Mackenzie provided the financial genius and Donald Mann the dreams.

He promised to build a big hotel in Vancouver, to operate a trans-Pacific shipping line, and create a coast steamship service to rival the C.P.R. and G.T.P. He organized a trans-Atlantic passenger service with the liners *Royal Edward* and *Royal George* between Avonmouth and Montreal. Known as Canadian Northern Steamships Ltd., it was to compete with the C.P.R.'s Atlantic Empresses. He started an emigrant service from Antwerp to Montreal with the Uranium Steamship Company, hoping to people the vast expanses of the prairies opened up by his new railway.

The last spike of the Mackenzie and Mann transcontinental line was driven on January 22, 1915, at Basque, B.C., near Ashcroft on the Thompson River. It was a hollow victory. Like the Grand Trunk Pacific, the Canadian Northern Pacific was insolvent, and the Mackenzie and Mann dream had become a load of debt. In return for aid given, the Dominion government demanded all the shares of the company.

On November 16, 1917, Canada took over nominal control of the Canadian Northern railway system, which was authorized to use the descriptive term Canadian National Railways. On June 6, 1919, the Canadian National Railway Company was incorporated for the purpose of "managing and operating a national system of railways." On August 23, 1920, the Grand Trunk Pacific was turned over to the Canadian Northern board for operation, and on January 30, 1923, became a part of the growing Canadian National Railways system. The B.C. coast steamship services of the G.T.P. remained under the same management, with Captain C. H. Nicholson in charge. On February 26, 1925, Grand Trunk Pacific Steamship Company formally became part of the Canadian National system. The high standard of operation was maintained.

Handsome red, white and blue funnel colors were adapted for the fleet, a marked improvement over the drab black of the G.T.P. The house flag became a red, white and blue pennant, with a red maple leaf in a white circle, surrounded by a wreath of maple leaves, surmounted by a crown. The new name of the company was Canadian National Steamships Ltd.

The bankruptcy of the Grand Trunk Railway system in 1916, and its takeover by the Canadian government, had little effect on the operations of the Pacific coast fleet. Indeed, World War One proved of advantage to the company for it created a boom in traffic to and from the Queen Charlotte Islands. This traffic was due to the sudden demand in 1918 for spruce lumber by the British government for construction of the primitive planes of the Royal Flying Corps. The Islands had vast stands of spruce and huge logging camps were built by the Imperial Munitions Board of Great Britain, as well as two big steam tugs, *Masset* and *Moresby*, to tow log booms to the Mainland.

The G.T.P. sold their ancient tug *Escort No. 2* in 1914 and replaced her in 1917 with the *Lorne*, built in 1897 by Robert Dunsmuir and Sons to tow coal ships out of Nanaimo. She had been owned since 1904 by the Puget Sound Tug Boat Company under the Canadian flag. She was resold in 1920 to the Hecate Straits Towing Company Ltd., owned by Captain B. L. Johnson. *Escort No. 2* was dismantled in 1918 and her machinery placed in the steam schooner *H. B. Lovejoy*. The hull of the ancient tug, built at Marshfield, Oregon, in 1882 was still sound, and was converted into a fish gathering barge.

The floating drydock, long promised for Prince Rupert, was completed in 1916 and turned over to the Grand Trunk Pacific for management under the name of Prince Rupert Dry Dock and Shipyard Company Ltd. It was the only dry dock in British Columbia at that time capable of handling ships of the Royal Navy then operating in the western Pacific. H.M.S. *Lancaster* was drydocked there for cleaning and painting in August 1916 and, in October 1917, the former Orient liner H.M.S. *Otranto*, then an armed merchant cruiser, went in for repairs under supervision of Yarrows Ltd. of Victoria. After the Grand Trunk Pacific had been taken over by the Dominion government, a sub-contract was given to an American firm to build two 8,000-ton freighters for the Canadian Government Merchant Marine Ltd.

Prince Rupert really didn't have the men or the facilities to build such sophisticated ships, and the American firm soon went bankrupt. The Wallace Shipyard of North Vancouver had to be called upon to take over the job, and the 400-foot *Canadian Britisher* and *Canadian Scottish* were not completed until 1921, at great cost to the Canadian taxpayer. In the years that followed, the great Prince Rupert dry dock was idle most of the time. Costs were high and it subsisted by occasional repair jobs for government-owned vessels. No ocean-going vessel was built until 1942. Throughout World War One the Prince Rupert dry dock was used only six times and that was for over-size naval craft which Esquimalt couldn't handle. No commerical craft was accommodated.

Vessels of the Mackenzie Brothers fleet had been purchased by the G.T.P. in 1910. The ancient *Henriette* continued to operate as a freighter until 1916 when she was sold to James Griffiths and Sons of Seattle who re-rigged her as a four-masted schooner for carrying ore from the Anyox and Britannia mines in B.C. to the Tacoma smelter. The Great War brought an acute shortage of tonnage and Griffiths sold her to French owners in Tahiti. She again flew the tricolor, as had been the case before her stranding in 1901. She remained active until 1922 when, on August 16, she was wrecked on Nukalaila Island in the Ellice group while on a voyage from Fiji to San Francisco with copra.

Another former member of the Mackenzie fleet which came to grief was the car barge *Georgian* which broke away from *Escort No. 2* in Queen Charlotte Sound on November 21, 1913. The tug, while searching for the barge, which had two men aboard, became disabled and was taken in tow by the Alaska steamer *Humboldt*. The *Georgian* was driven ashore and became a total loss, but the two men were picked up by search vessels.

In 1917 the Grand Trunk increased its fleet

with the purchase of the wooden motor schooner *Tillamook*, built in 1911 by Kruse and Banks of North Bend, Oregon. The G.T.P. planned to use her in the fish trade between Ketchikan and Seattle under an American-flag subsidiary called Grand Trunk Pacific Alaska S.S. Company Inc. She was rebuilt with a shelter deck that raised her tonnage to 615. Her dimensions were 125 feet overall by 28 feet beam, and she was powered by twin 175 h.p. Frisco Standard gas engines which gave her a speed of 10 knots. She had accommodation for 27 passengers, but she was not a success. She lay idle at the Grand Trunk Dock in Vancouver for several years until she was sold in 1925 to Northland Transportation Company of Seattle and renamed *Norco* for the Ketchikan run. She was wrecked on March 8, 1944, on Annette Island, Alaska.

The Canadian National system received a dynamic new president and chairman of the board in 1922. He was Sir Henry Thornton, another American-born railwayman who had made his reputation in Great Britain. He set out to revive the moribund C.N.R., with money no problem. On the West Coast one of his first actions in 1923 was to discontinue the money-losing triangle service between Vancouver, Victoria and Seattle.

One of the commitments made by Mackenzie and Mann had been to build fast ships to compete with the C.P.R. and G.T.P. on the triangle run. Even after the Canadian Northern was bankrupt and taken over by the Canadian government, Honorable C. C. Ballantyne, Federal Minister of Marine, had announced that he expected to call for tenders on January 1, 1920, for two fast vessels for the run for Canadian National. He said they were to be 50 feet longer than the C.P.R. ships and several knots faster. Nothing came of these extravagant plans until they were revived in 1928 by Sir Henry Thorn-

ton. In that year he also created Canadian National Steamships (West Indies) Ltd. on the East Coast, with a fleet of five fine passenger ships with the prefix "Lady," such as *Lady Nelson*. They ran to Bermuda and the West Indies.

In 1925 an additional passenger vessel was added to the former G.T.P. fleet for Queen Charlotte Islands service. Captain Dan Donald went to Scotland for the company and purchased the fine little liner *St. Margaret*, built in 1907 by the Ailsa Shipbuilding Company of Ayr, Scotland. She was 1,344 gross tons, 242 feet by 33 feet, licensed for 178 berthed passengers, with 150 tons cargo capacity.

Her original owners were David MacBrayne Ltd. of Glasgow. As the *Chieftain*, she had operated a passenger and mail service to the Outer Hebrides. She had fine lines and was noteworthy for her clipper bow and figurehead — a highland chieftain in full regalia. She had been sold to the North of Scotland, Orkney and Shetland Steam Navigation Company for the run from Aberdeen to the northern islands and renamed *St. Margaret*. Since she was designed for the stormy seas off the coasts of Scotland, she was suitable for the similar run off the British Columbia coast. She was to give 20 years of sterling service as *Prince Charles*, and later as *Camosun*. Unfortunately, her figurehead was removed for her B.C. service.

She was originally a coal burner, and on her way out to B.C. she ran so short of fuel she had to burn all the cattle stalls that were still on the ship in order to keep up steam. When she arrived in Nanaimo there was only one little nugget of coal.

I travelled in the comfortable old vessel in September 1941 between Prince Rupert and the Queen Charlotte Islands. A Royal Canadian Air Force station had recently been established at Alliford Harbour, near Skidegate, and there was

The *Prince William* was originally built for the German navy. She was not a success on the B.C. coast.

a detachment of young airmen aboard. *Prince Charles* had been purchased recently by the Union Steamship Company, and was now the *Camosun*, but her old Canadian National crew, under Captain James Watt, was still in charge.

It was a period of great emotional strain, for the Battle of Britain had reached its peak. At the same time the German army was marshalling its forces on the channel coast in "Operation Sea Lion," the projected invasion of the British Isles.

One of the passengers on *Camosun* was a French priest who had a remote parish on the Queen Charlotte Islands. This sinister man button-holed each passenger, and said he was a student of the prophesies of St. Anthony of Padua. "The swastika will fly over Buckingham

Palace tomorrow morning," he announced. Some Air Force boys then threatened to throw him overboard. When word of this threat came to Captain Watt, he told the priest that if he uttered another word of defeatism, he'd put him in irons. That improved morale aboard ship enormously.

Another ship arrived in 1930 to supplement the service from Prince Rupert to the Queen Charlottes, and was renamed *Prince William*. It is difficult to understand why she was purchased for she proved quite unsuitable for the short, stormy run across Hecate Strait. She was 177 feet long by 24 feet beam, and 409 gross tons. She was built in 1915 by the Neptun shipyard at Rostock, Germany, as the minesweeper M-10 for the Imperial German Navy. After the war she was converted to the passenger ship *Aktion*.

Prince William was refitted at Prince Rupert, but she operated for barely a year before she was laid up. Her German engines gave constant trouble and she became known locally as "Smokey Willie." With a narrow beam and shallow draft, her gyrations in the stormy waters made her most unpopular. After a long lay-up at Prince Rupert she was sold in 1937 to Captain Paul Armour who intended to convert her to a salvage tug. However, he never used her and in 1939 he broke her up at Prince Rupert, unhonored and unsung.

Arrival of *Prince Charles* made *Prince Albert*, ex *Bruno* of 1892, redundant, and in 1925 she was sold to a Vancouver rum-running syndicate without change of name. For many years she acted as a mother ship, loading cargoes of liquor at Vancouver, Tahiti or Antwerp. She would then lie outside the California 12-mile limit to off-load her cargo into fast speed boats. She soon ran into trouble. In April 1925, when lying off San Francisco, she fouled the Pacific cable, breaking communication with the Orient. She was promptly sued for damages by the Commercial Cable Company. Her owners avoided payment by transferring her to another dummy company.

After prohibition ended in the United States in 1933 her rum-running days were over. She was sold to the Badwater Towing Company, converted to a towboat and returned to the Queen Charlotte Islands as *J. R. Morgan*, towing Davis rafts to the Mainland. At age 57 she was converted to a log barge by the Tahsis Company and foundered in May 1950 off the west coast of Vancouver Island when her cargo shifted in a storm.

Between World War One and World War Two the port of Prince Rupert was a quiet backwater, almost forgotten by the world. During the de-

pression years the population sank to about 6,000, far below the optimistic 50,000 of C. M. Hays' dreams. The floating dry dock was mostly idle, and the town relied almost entirely on the fishing industry for survival. The Grand Trunk Pacific Railway was now a mere branch line of the Canadian National. The grand hotel project was still only a hole in the ground, with many of the streets still muddy and unpaved. In 1933 the city went bankrupt and was unable to pay the interest on its bonds until 1943.

Prince Rupert, however, had one industry that thrived. The city had a big surplus of unmarried men, so a restricted "red light" district was established to meet their carnal needs. Known locally as "The Hump," it consisted of a string of cottages on Comox Avenue at the back of town. A brightly lit boardwalk ran down the center of the street, often called the "Great White Way." Each cottage had two bow windows, in each of which sat a professional lady demurely knitting or reading a book. A prospective customer could then stroll along the boardwalk and window-shop.

The Hump was strictly controlled and the girls were allowed into the downtown area only to do their shopping on Thursdays. On that day respectable matrons stayed home.

The madam in charge of the operation was Blanche Hart, known and respected far and wide on the B.C. coast. When she died the mayor and aldermen were mourners at her funeral, which almost became a civic event. A story was told of the high standards of the facility. On one occasion a fisherman went "Over the Hump" with his entire season's earnings in his wallet. When he sobered up in the morning his money was missing and he complained to the police chief. He was sent to Madame Blanche who produced his wallet with the contents intact. She then gave him a dressing-down for carrying so much money.

"It puts temptation in the way of the girls," she said.

The Hump continued to flourish until the American Army arrived at Prince Rupert in 1942 to establish a staging post for the Alaska campaign. Ever mindful of the morals of their men, the prudish Yanks ordered the local authorities to close down Comox Avenue. It never reopened after the war, and a great tradition disappeared.

Prince Rupert awoke from its slumbers with abrupt suddenness after Pearl Harbor in December 1942. The Americans quickly realized its strategic importance, with its magnificent harbour and railway connections, and thousands of troops were based there, along with attendant barracks and facilities necessary for a staging post. The population grew to about 24,000, and was at the bursting point.

The dormant shipyard and dry dock came to life with needed repairs to American army vessels, and a new shipbuilding program was augmented by the Canadian government.

During the war years four "Bangor" class minesweepers were built for the Royal Canadian Navy, 13 dry cargo ships of the 10,000 deadweight ton "Fort" and "Park" classes, and two, 224 foot China coasters.

There was a gala day in Prince Rupert in September 1943 when the new "Algerine" class frigate, H.M.C.S. *Prince Rupert*, paid a courtesy visit to her namesake city under command of Lieutenant-Commander R. W. Draney. Citizens had the opportunity to view "their own ship" before she set sail for Halifax. She joined escort group C-3 on the St. John's, Newfoundland,

mid-ocean run. While with her second westbound convoy on March 13, 1944, she assisted with the kill of a German submarine, *U-575*, 400 miles north of the Azores. After the war, H.M.C.S. *Prince Rupert* returned to Esquimalt and ended her days as part of a breakwater on the beach at Royston, near Comox. She was one of 17 frigates built by Yarrows Ltd. at Esquimalt between 1942 and 1944.

There was another vessel called *Prince Rupert*, which was intended for passenger service in British Columbia waters. In 1893 a fast steel sidewheeler was ordered by the Canadian Pacific Railway for the run between Vancouver and Victoria, but she never reached her intended destination. The 270-foot *Prince Rupert* was completed by the famous yard of Denny's of Dumbarton, Scotland. She was to compete with the *Islander* of 1888, built in Scotland for the Canadian Pacific Navigation Company of Victoria, which at that time had no connection with the C.P.R.

Prince Rupert was a handsome, flush-decked little ship of 1,158 tons gross, with comfortable passenger accommodation. She left Great Britain in September 1894 bound for Vancouver. Meanwhile, Victoria interests had managed to arouse a local uproar and C.P.R. directors decided it would be prudent to change their plans. When the ship reached Tenerife, in the Canary Islands to coal, she received orders to return to Britain.

After a short lay-up at Plymouth, she was turned over to a C.P.R. subsidiary, the Dominion Atlantic Railway, and for nearly 20 years ran successfully on the Bay of Fundy between Digby and Saint John.

CHAPTER SIX

The *Prince Robert*, one of the finest coastal passenger liners ever to sail Pacific Northwest waters.

Queens of the North

Soon after Sir Henry Thornton took over the helm as president and chairman of the Canadian National system, he announced grandiose plans for the future. Vancouver Island was to have a new railway line between Victoria and Patricia Bay, as promised by Mackenzie and Mann. The old Grand Trunk pier at Vancouver would be replaced by a new passenger terminal. In the spring of 1928 he announced orders would be placed for three luxury liners for West Coast service, each to be about 5,500 tons gross, with a speed of 22 knots. The tri-city run would be restored and one ship would be devoted to luxury cruises to Alaska which would be marketed world-wide.

Mackenzie and Mann had been particularly interested in the natural wealth of Vancouver Island. In 1910 they had paid $11 million for Canadian Collieries (Dunsmuir) Ltd., which controlled the coal wealth of the Island. In the same year they promoted Canadian North Pacific Fisheries Ltd., with whaling stations on the west coast of Vancouver Island and the Queen Charlotte Islands. In addition, through their major interest in the Canadian Western Lumber Company, they controlled huge timber limits on Vancouver Island, and the largest sawmill in the province at Fraser Mills near New Westminster.

In 1913 they guaranteed to build a new luxury hotel at Vancouver within five years, and start a trans-Pacific passenger service within eight years. As a sideline, by November 1911, 13 miles of track was built eastward from Stewart in Northwestern B.C. by a subsidiary called Canadian Northeastern Railway Company. It was intended to connect with the Grand Trunk Pacific, and to tap the rich mineral wealth of northern British Columbia. Most of these dreams faded, both on land and water.

The Canadian Northern Pacific Railway was unable to secure a right-of-way into the port of Vancouver, so trackage rights were acquired from the Great Northern Railway. To this day, the Canadian National Railway runs into Vancouver on the tracks of the Burlington Northern, successor to the Great Northern. The Canadian Northern acquired yards through an extensive land fill at the head of False Creek in Burrard Inlet, and completed a handsome terminal station in 1918.

The actual physical terminus of C.N. tracks was established at Port Mann on the south bank of the Fraser River several miles above New Westminster. In order to provide a link between the company's new Victoria to Patricia Bay line on Vancouver Island and Port Mann, the Canadian Northern ordered the train and passenger ferry *Canora* from the Davie Shipbuilding and Repair Company of Lauzon, Quebec. She was a vessel of 2,383 gross tons, 940 net tons, 308 feet by 52.1 by 18.8, and was launched on June 10, 1918. Powered with a four-cylinder, triple expansion engine developing 2,200 i.h.p., she was a double-ender with two propellers at each end. She was designed to carry passengers but the accommodation was never completed. Registered at Quebec under the ownership of Canadian Northern Steamship Company Ltd., she carried their funnel colors — buff, with a broad blue band and a black top. On the blue band was a black flag with the letters C.N.R. in white, placed diagonally on the flag.

A few days before she was to leave for the west coast she was rammed on the port bow by the Canadian Pacific liner *Sicilian* and it was several weeks before she was repaired. She left Quebec City on September 29, 1918, calling at Sydney, Halifax, Panama and California for bunkers, and arrived at Victoria on December 7, 1918. War was still on when she sailed and she had been fitted at Halifax with a four-inch gun on her stern, and carried three Royal Navy gunners. She also brought supplies for the naval base at Esquimalt. The ship was opened for public inspection, a Victoria newspaper exhuberantly noting: "The arrival of the *Canora* marks a new approach to the development of transportation, and her advent will play a very important part in building up Victoria as one of the foremost ports of the Pacific."

After a refit she made her initial trip between Port Mann and Patricia Bay on April 30, 1919, taking five and a half hours. *Canora* also made occasional calls at Nanaimo to load coal cars for the mainland for use on C.N. trains.

A car barge towing service from Port Mann to Vancouver Island had started in 1916 and was maintained by two whale-catcher vessels preempted from the Canadian North Pacific Fisheries Ltd. fleet and converted into tugboats. They were the *Sebastian* and *Germania*, which were renamed *Saanich* and *Fraser*. They were near sisters, both built by the Akers shipyard in Christiania (Oslo) in 1904 and 1903 respectively.

Sebastian, which had been purchased in Newfoundland, arrived at Victoria in the spring of 1910. The 103 ton chaser boat measured 93.5 feet by 16.8 by 10.3. *Germania* arrived the same year from the Chilean whaling grounds. She

Sir Henry Thornton, and Sir Donald Mann. Thornton's dreams included an impressive hotel in Vancouver which he named after himself. When the hotel finally opened in 1939, Thornton had been fired and the Hotel Thornton became today's familiar Hotel Vancouver.

Below: Victoria Harbour in the 1920s, the Grand Trunk wharf at right with both the *Prince George* and the *Prince Rupert* in port.

measured 94.3 feet by 16.8 by 10, and 106 gross tons.

Fraser ended her days as *Canadian National No. 4* for Canadian Northern Steamships Ltd., but *Saanich* was to return briefly as a whale catcher. Purchased by Coastal Towing Company Ltd., in 1948, she was resold the same year to B.C. Packers Ltd. for operation out of their whaling station at Coal Harbour in Quatsino Sound. However, she was soon found to be too old for the purpose and was sold for scrap.

In 1928 Canadian National Railways augmented the tug and barge service with two powerful tugs which they named *Canadian National No. 1* and *Canadian National No. 2*. The former was originally the British Admiralty tug *Finwale*, built at Middlesbrough, England, in 1915, 125 feet long. She had been brought to British Columbia in 1923 and operated by Hopkins Brothers of Hopkins Landing under the name *Hopkins Bros*.

Canadian National No. 2 was originally *St. Catherine*, 135.5 feet long, one of 64 "Saint" class rescue tugs ordered by the Royal Navy for convoy duty during the First World War. Her triple expansion engines developed, 1,250 h.p. and could manage 12 knots when running free. She was purchased in England in 1926 by Vancouver's harbor master, Captain A. H. Reed, for use as a fireboat, at a cost of $54,000. She lay idle for two years until she was transferred to the C.N.R. in 1928 and renamed.

Two sister ships also came to British Columbia. *St. Florence*, later *Kyuquot*, was acquired by the Canadian Pacific Railway in 1924 for their car-barge service, and *St. Faith*, later *S. D. Brooks*, was purchased by Kingcome Navigation Company Ltd. in 1926, and was employed towing log barges.

These powerful steam tugs proved very successful. In February 1942 *Canadian National No. 2* and *Kyuquot* were called upon to assist in the drydocking at Esquimalt of the *Queen Elizabeth*, the world's largest liner. Then on trooping duties, she eventually carried 15,000 troops at a time. The assignment included assisting the liner when she was at anchor so she would swing properly on the tides at Royal Roads and English Bay.

Canadian National No. 2 continued to give good service until 1961 when the C.N.R. built a new ferry slip at Tilbury Island, 12½ miles down river from Port Mann. The new facility cut a considerable amount of time off the car ferry run and, with declining traffic to Vancouver Island, made her redundant. On April 24, 1963, she docked at Tilbury Island slip for the last time. The tug was sold to a scrap dealer but her service was far from over. In mid-1964 she was purchased by North Pacific Towing and Salvage Company Ltd., given a thorough overhaul and renamed *Polaris*. She operated on several long distance towing jobs until 1968 when Gulf of Georgia Towing Company Ltd. purchased her and renamed her *Gulf Freda*. For a time she operated on the railway car barge service between Prince Rupert and Whittier, Alaska. She was dismantled at Tacoma in 1983.

Canora operated regularly on the Port Mann service until 1932 when the depression caused her lay-up until 1937. During World War Two she was again fitted with a gun, painted grey, and continued to make regular trips to Victoria, carrying rail cars with supplies for the two shipyards there. She was laid up in Vancouver in May 1967 awaiting sale. In recent years her speed had dropped from 14 knots to 10.

Sold to a Victoria scrap dealer in April 1968, she was resold to Goodwin Johnson Ltd. of Vancouver for use as a pontoon at their loading facility in Upper Burrard Inlet. At one time it was announced that she would be towed to the

Queen Charlotte Islands and converted to a floating sawmill, but nothing came of it and her sad remains are still afloat. Her antique triple expansion engines were donated to a museum at Chilliwack, B.C., in 1985.

After the retirement of *Canora* the rail barge service on the Fraser was maintained by chartered tugs towing C.N. transfer barges. The chartered, self-propelled rail car ferry, *Greg Yorke*, of F. M. Yorke and Son Ltd. of Vancouver, took over the service from Tilbury Island to Victoria from 1968 to April 1988 when the service ended after nearly 72 years and *Seaspan Greg*, ex *Greg Yorke*, was withdrawn.

The three new ships promised for the Pacific coast by Sir Henry Thornton were ordered in 1929 from Cammell Laird & Company of Birkenhead, who had previously built the successful "Lady" ships for the West Indies service of Canadian National Steamships. They were intended to be the finest ships on the British Columbia coast, to operate on the triangle run and to Alaska. It was expected they would compete fiercely with the rival Canadian Pacific ships. They were also designed for conversion to naval use in time of war. Cammell Laird demurred at the plans, which they considered unsuitable for West Coast service. They were overruled, but as events were to prove, they were right.

The ships were christened *Prince Henry, Prince David* and *Prince Robert*, not after royal princes, but after Sir Henry Thornton himself and his two vice-presidents. In addition, the new Canadian National hotel under construction at Vancouver apparantly was to be named the Hotel Thornton, but it was not to be. The time was not right for either the ships or the hotel, and the great depression delayed completion of the hotel. It opened in 1939 — as today's familiar Hotel Vancouver.

First of the trio of new ships was *Prince Henry*, christened by Miss Ishbel MacDonald, daughter of the British Prime Minster. The vessel arrived at Vancouver on June 21, 1930, followed shortly by *Prince David. Prince Robert* did not arrive until May 1931, having had to return to her builders with engine trouble. *Prince Henry* was opened to public inspection on her arrival at Vancouver and her magnificent accommodation brought much favorable comment. No expense had been spared in her fitting out, and she and her sisters cost about $2 million each. A new passenger pier was built at Vancouver to service the liners but it was completely destroyed by fire on August 10, 1930, soon after the arrival of the first ship. It was an inauspicious start for the new services.

Prince Henry and her sisters had accommodation for 334 first-class and 70 third-class passengers each, and had certificates for 1,500 passengers on day trips. Like their earlier consorts, the new Princes had three closely-spaced funnels in the company colors — red with a white band and a dark blue top. Gross tonnage was 6,893 and net 3,054. Length was 364.6 feet overall with a beam of 57.1 feet. Loaded draft was 16.6 feet. Twin engines were driven by Parsons turbines, giving an official speed of 20 knots at about 19,000 shaft horsepower, but the ships often made 22, and *Prince Henry* reached 23 on her trials.

Their pile-up of six decks gave them a rather clumsy appearance, without the grace of their C.P.R. rivals. *Prince Henry* entered the Alaska cruise service on July 3, 1930, while *Prince David* re-established the tri-city run between Vancouver, Victoria and Seattle on August 12. With the arrival of *Prince Robert* in 1931, a daily sailing each way was established. but it was only to last one summer. The new ships consistently lost money.

They soon proved they had deficiencies in

The *Prince Henry* and, at bottom, the *Prince David*.

their design. They were high-sided and less manoeuvrable than the Princesses and required tugs for berthing and un-berthing in the narrow confines of Victoria's inner harbour. They were expensive to run and created no new business, but simply took some of the traffic away from the C.P.R. opposition. When travelling at speed they created a tremendous wash which caused so much damage to sea walls in West Vancouver they were forced to reduce speed to 10 knots in Burrard Inlet.

In July 1931 *Prince Robert* ran aground near Port Townsend and had to be withdrawn from service. On September 5, 1931, the Canadian National tri-city service was ended forever. The expensive new ships had proved a dismal failure. Work on the magnificent C.N. hotel at Vancouver was suspended and it was to lie idle until its completion in 1939. *Prince Henry* and *Prince David* were sent to the Atlantic coast to operate as cruise liners. *Prince Robert* remained laid up in Vancouver until the summer of 1935 when she made four, eleven-day cruises to Alaska under Captain H. E. Nedden. During the three-day layovers in Vancouver she made a series of popular two-day or afternoon cruises. Meanwhile, the extravagance of Sir Henry Thornton and the failure of his new ships brought the wrath of the new Conservative government on his shoulders. He was dismissed as president of the Canadian National system, all his dreams in ruins and his new hotel uncompleted. As noted, it was subsequently to become the Hotel Vancouver, jointly operated by the C.N.R. and C.P.R., and is now owned by the C.P.R.

Prince Robert, however, did have a day of glory in the summer of 1939 when she was chosen to serve as royal yacht during the visit of King George VI and Queen Elizabeth to British Columbia. She brought the royal party to Vancouver from Victoria, accompanied by a naval escort. She also established a record for the trip, three hours and ten minutes from Brotchie Ledge to Point Grey bell buoy, a distance of 72 nautical miles.

When *Prince Henry* and *Prince David* commenced their Atlantic cruising in 1932, it was the depth of the depression and it is doubtful if either made a profit. In late 1932 *Prince Henry* made 24 round trips from Boston to West Indies ports and Havana. After a lay-up at Halifax she made five Caribbean cruises and one cruise under charter back to the Pacific, passing through the Panama Canal, up the coast to Skagway, and returning via Honolulu. In 1937 she was chartered to Clarke Steamship Company of Quebec who cruised her out of the St. Lawrence in the summer and Miami to Port au Prince, Kingston and Havana in the winter. She was purchased outright by the Clarke Company in 1938 and re-named *North Star*. Her new colors were white hull, and yellow funnels with four narrow, closely-spaced light blue bands.

Prince David, the unlucky member of the trio, came to grief early in her cruising career when she ran aground in 1932 on a Bermuda reef. There were no casualties, but at first it was feared she would be a total loss. Eventually she was salvaged and returned to service as a cruise vessel after an expensive repair job. She also sailed with a white hull but retained C.N. funnel colors.

CHAPTER SEVEN

The Princes go to War

Declaration of war on September 3, 1939, meant the end of luxury cruising for the three ships. Early in that month the Canadian Naval Service informed the British Admiralty that they were available for war use. The Royal Navy replied on September 26 that two of them might be requisitioned and fitted out with equipment that had been accumulating in Canada since 1937. Meanwhile, proceedings began for taking over the *David* and the *Robert* on a charter basis from the railway. Outright purchase was recommended by the Chief of Naval Staff on December 8, 1939, in which he proposed that they be incorporated in the permanent navy. *Prince Robert* was transferred to the Royal Canadian Navy at Esquimalt and *Prince David* at Halifax on February 5, 1940. The final purchase price was more than $700,000 each. *North Star* was transferred on March 11 at Halifax for more than $800,000 and reverted to her original name as H.M.C.S. *Prince Henry*. The conversion cost was $763,000 for *Prince David* at Halifax Shipyards, $755,300 for *Prince Robert* at Burrard Dry Dock in Vancouver, and $815,900 for *Prince Henry* at Canadian Vickers in Montreal.

I recall seeing *Prince Robert* being stripped of her passenger accommodation in Vancouver. It was pouring rain and all her magnificent furnishings, carpets, bedding, and even the sterling

The *Prince Robert* and, opposite page, the *Prince David* as Canadian navy merchant cruisers in World War Two.

silver champagne buckets were unceremoniously tossed into a soggy heap on the dockside. Work on the *Robert* was completed by the end of July 1940, but the *David* and the *Henry* were not ready until the end of the year. They were found to be in much worse condition than the *Robert* and much extra time and money had to be spent on their hulls and machinery.

The conversions consisted of cutting away the two top decks and fitting a light cruiser superstructure. The two forward funnels were removed and the uptakes trunked into one very large diameter funnel. The hulls and decks had to be stiffened, accommodation arrangements revised and watertight subdivisions greatly extended. The armament consisted of two, six-inch guns forward and two aft; two, three-inch anti-aircraft guns amidships and depth charges at the stern.

As armed merchant cruisers they possessed many faults. They had a very rapid and jerky roll, a great disadvantage for gun-laying. The guns were inadequate. The main six-inch guns dated back to the Boer War and the three-inch guns came from light cruisers of 1916-18 vintage.

Prince Robert was the first to see action. While she was lying at Esquimalt in September 1940 intelligence was received that the German freighter *Weser*, lying interned at Manzanillo, Mexico, planned to make a break-out. *Prince Robert* still required stores, a shakedown cruise and training of her raw crew. Yet at dawn on September 12 she sailed for Manzanillo in a very unready state. She patrolled off the port for a week, keeping out of sight during the day and closing into binocular range at night.

After dark on September 25 she had taken up her usual in-shore station when she sighted *Weser* coming out of Manzanillo Bay. *Prince*

Robert ran as close inshore as she dared so that her silhouette in the darkness was obscured as much as possible. *Weser* continued on her course on the impression that the *Robert* was a Mexican gunboat. After stalking the quarry until she was outside the three-mile limit, the warship churned up alongside *Weser's* port quarter, her searchlight ablaze. The freighter stopped at a shouted order and within minutes a party from *Prince Robert* was aboard. There was no trouble with the startled German crew and *Weser* was escorted to Esquimalt with the White Ensign flying above the swastika, the first important Canadian prize of war. She was renamed *Vancouver Island* and was later torpedoed in the North Atlantic on October 15, 1941, with the loss of all on board.

Prince Robert soon began a series of escort cruises bringing New Zealand and Australian airmen to Canada for training. In 1941 she escorted the liner *Awatea* from Vancouver to Hong Kong with Canadian troops destined to be captured by the Japanese. She cleared Honolulu for home just three days before the attack on Pearl Harbor. She was in Sydney, Australia, when the Japanese surrendered and was the first ship to send a landing party to Sham Shui prison camp at Hong Kong where 370 Canadians were among the 1,500 internees.

Prince Henry was commissioned at Halifax in December 1940 and on March 31, 1941, was cruising in the Pacific off Callao with the cruiser H.M.S. *Diomede*. Two German freighters, *Harmonthis* and *Muenchen*, attempted to escape the blockade. Both freighters fled in different directions, but when overhauled they were set on fire. For four hours an engine-room party from *Prince Henry* fought the fire on *Harmonthis* until the Canadian warship was forced to sink her by gunfire. *Muenchen* was sunk by a Peruvian cruiser.

On August 20, 1942, the three Canadian armed merchant cruisers, with corvettes *Dawson* and *Vancouver*, sailed from Esquimalt for Kodiak, Alaska. There, under orders from the United States Navy, they escorted convoys from Kodiak to Dutch Harbor for over two months under foul conditions of fog and gales, with the Aleutian williwaws roaring down the narrow passes from the Bering Sea. Up to this time the U.S. Navy was unequipped for convoy duty and relied on Canadian ships in Alaska and West Indies waters. The three Canadian armed merchant cruisers returned from the north at the end of October.

In 1942 authorities finally admitted that the three Princes were no longer suitable to serve in their current role. It was decided to re-arm the *Robert* as an auxiliary anti-air cruiser, and to convert the other two to L.S.I. (M)'s (Landing Ships Infantry.) The change was approved early in 1943, the work done at Burrard Dry Dock in Vancouver. The *Robert's* new armament consisted of 10, four-inch guns on twin mountings; two, two-pounder quadruple pom-poms; and 12 Oerlikons, making her one of the most powerful A/A ships of her size afloat.

Prince Henry and *Prince David* each carried four, four-inch guns, two single Bofors, and 10 Oerlikons. Each also carried eight minor landing craft, could accommodate 550 army personnel and had a complement of 31 officers and 322 seamen. On their arrival in the United Kingdom their conversion was finished at the John Brown shipyard on the Clyde. Radar was fitted and they were made ready for the Normandy invasion. *Prince Henry* was delegated to be Headquarters ship on Juno Beach and was reviewed by King George VI on May 24, 1944. She embarked 362 assault troops of the Canadian Scottish Regiment of Victoria and *Prince David* embarked 400 troops of the Regiment de la Chaudiere.

Both ships later took part in Operation Dragoon in the Mediterranean, landing troops at Port Cros, 22 miles east of Toulon, on August 15. *Prince Henry* served as the flagship of Rear-Admiral T. E. Chandler of the United States Navy, who commanded the main division of the invasion. In the follow-up operations both Princes made several trips to Corsica.

In September and October 1944 *Prince Henry* and *Prince David* both played a big part in the liberation of Greece. The former made several trips with refugees from the Adriatic coast to Taranto, with the ship sometimes being shelled from hidden strongholds ashore. The prime minister of Greece and members of the government embarked at Taranto on October 14, landing on Greek soil at Piraeus on October 17. After further transport duties, *Prince Henry* proceeded to London in March 1945 where she was paid off as a Canadian ship. After the fall of Japan she was laid up at Falmouth where she was sold to the British Ministry of War Transport.

Renamed *Empire Parkeston*, she was converted at Southampton into a cross-channel ferry and put on trooping service between Harwich and the Hook of Holland, carrying men on leave and replacements between Britain and the British Army of Occupation. She was laid up in 1961 and scrapped next year in Italy, aged 31.

Prince David, the unlucky ship of the trio, managed to strike a mine in the Aegean during her Mediterranean adventure, but the damage was superficial. She was later sent back to Esquimalt in anticipation of taking part in the Far East campaign, but after Japan surrendered she and *Prince Robert* were decommissioned and laid up in Bedwell Bay at the upper end of Burrard Inlet. There was a keen demand in those days for any passenger liner that could float and the two Canadian National ships were soon purchased by the Charlton Steamship Company Ltd., owned by Chandris Brothers, a well-known firm of London Greeks. They were renamed *Charlton Monarch* and *Charlton Sovereign* respectively and early in 1947 sailed for Southampton under their own power. The unlucky *Monarch*, ex *Prince David*, distinguished herself en route by catching fire at Curacao while re-fuelling.

After a refit at Antwerp to carry passengers under spartan conditions, they were time-char-

Aerial view of Prince Rupert
in the 1970s, the Provincial
Government building in the crescent.

tered in May 1948 to the International Refugee Organization for transporting displaced persons and refugees from Europe. Each could now accommodate 750 passengers in eight-berth cabins and in dormitories for 20 to 40 people.

In May 1948 the *Monarch* left Bremerhaven with refugees for Buenos Aires. She put into St. Vincent, Cape Verde, with boiler trouble and later was towed into Pernambuco after an engine breakdown. Years of vigorous service in the Canadian Navy were taking their toll. The passengers were removed and in July the tug *Zealandia* took her in tow for Great Britain. Even the tug broke down with engine trouble, and another tug took over at Las Palmas. She was finally delivered to the Clyde on October 1. *Charlton Monarch*, after only one inglorious voyage, was laid up in Wales and in June 1948 was abandoned to the underwriters. She was scrapped at Newport, Wales, in 1951, a very expensive investment for Chandris Brothers.

Charlton Sovereign, ex *Prince Robert*, also had her share of engine trouble. She first sailed from Bremerhaven for Australia in August 1948, was delayed at Gibraltar with boiler trouble for almost a month and then at Batavia with engine defects. Her voyage to Sydney took no less that 86 days. Her second round voyage from Bremerhaven to Rio de Janeiro was also interrupted by engine trouble, and on her return she spent two months on the Tyne under repair. Once back in service she had better luck and made three round voyages from Naples to Rio, one from Naples to Halifax and one from Naples to Central America.

After some pilgrim voyages in 1951 she was sold to the Italian shipowners Grimaldi Brothers

of Genoa, who made a practice of buying ancient ships and restructuring them for the emigrant trades. After a lengthy rejuvenation, the former *Prince Robert* reappeared under the name *Lucania*, unrecognizable for her former self. The Italians have always shown a talent for producing a silk purse from a sow's ear and *Lucania* emerged as a handsome ship, externally and internally, with a white hull, two new well-placed funnels and a lengthened bow. She never looked better, and now accommodated 90 first class, 90 intermediate and 560 tourist passengers. She operated successfully in the emigrant trade between Italy and Venezuela until she was broken up near Leghorn in 1962, aged 32.

During the wartime years *Prince Rupert* and *Prince George* were kept busy on the Pacific coast, particularly after the United States Army took over the port of Prince Rupert in 1942 and used it as a staging post for the Alaska campaign. The two veteran steamers were the sole passenger ships remaining in the Canadian National fleet on the Pacific after June 1940 when the ships on the Queen Charlotte Islands service were sold to the Union Steamship Company of British Columbia Ltd. Despite a government subsidy, the ships had been losing money.

Prince Charles became *Camosun* (ii), and *Prince John* was renamed *Cassiar* (ii). Both were getting to be ancient mariners but they remained popular with the Islanders, and were particularly useful after a Royal Canadian Air Force base was established at Alliford Bay, near Skidegate Inlet, in 1941. This development brought a thousand men to the Islands overnight, in addition to the work crew building an air strip at Sandspit.

CHAPTER EIGHT

Back to Peacetime Service

After World War Two the Union company converted three British-built former corvettes into comfortable passenger ships and the old-timers became redundant. The former *Prince John* was sold for scrap, but there was still a market for the staunch former *Prince Charles* which had started life as *Chieftain* in the stormy waters of the Hebrides in 1907. She was purchased in late 1945 by the London-Greek firm of John Livanos and Sons, registered in Tel-Aviv, and sailed from Vancouver to the eastern Mediterranean under the name *Cairo*. It was suspected that she might participate in the illegal Jewish emigrant trade to Palestine, but apparently she kept on the right side of the law. Until early 1947 she ran regularly between Marseilles and Alexandria, via Haifa, with a passenger capacity of 194. Then she was switched to a new route from Marseilles to Mombasa and Beira, owned by another Livanos company, Zarati Steamship Company of Panama. She even made a few trans-Atlantic voyages from Marseilles to the southern Caribbean and remained in service until 1950. She was a remarkably successful little ship during her long and varied career.

Canadian National Steamship Company Ltd. further contracted their operations by selling the former Grand Trunk Dock at Seattle and, when *Prince George* burned at Ketchikan in September 1945, only *Prince Rupert* was left in service between Vancouver and Prince Rupert. In February 1946 she became the first commercial Canadian vessel to be equipped with radar.

The company was determined to remain in the lucrative tourist trade to Alaska, so a contract for a new *Prince George* was let in 1946 at a cost of $3 million to Yarrows Ltd. of Victoria. She was launched at their Esquimalt shipyard on October 6, 1947, and placed in service on the Alaska run in June 1948. She was designed by Vancouver naval architect W. D. McLaren, who had designed several of the passenger ships of the Union fleet, including the conversion of the three ex-corvettes. The new *Prince George* was a sturdy-looking ship, 5,812 gross tons, 335.1 feet long, 52.1 feet beam and 24.1 feet depth. She was a single-funnelled, twin-screw oil-burner powered by two, 12 cylinder Uniflow steam engines which gave her a service speed of 15.5 knots. There was accommodation for 368 first-class passengers.

The Alaska cruise season usually began in April and lasted until October each year. Ports of call northbound included Ketchikan, Juneau and Skagway, and southbound at Wrangell, Prince Rupert and Alert Bay. She was usually laid up during the winter months except while relieving *Prince Rupert* during her refit.

Prince George looked quite handsome with black hull, white upperworks and red white and blue Canadian National funnel. Unfortunately, in 1963 she was given new funnel colors which did nothing to improve her appearance. The funnel was then painted a hideous "box-car" vermilion red, on which was superimposed in white script the letters CN. The Princess ships of the C.P.R. followed this "modernization" in 1967 when they abandoned their traditional red-and-white checkered house flag and buff black-

The *Prince George* outbound under Vancouver's Lions Gate Bridge.

topped funnels. Replacing them was a weird meaningless design, dreamed up at great expense by a U.S. advertising agency, thus breaking the hearts of many C.P.R. old-timers.

The career of *Prince George* was uneventful and she built up a reputation for regularity and comfort. The gallant old *Prince Rupert* also maintained an uneventful career in her last years, except for her collision with *Princess Kathleen* in 1951. Shortly after the war she had been given a complete refit and reappeared with shorter funnels and a radar scanner on her foremast above her bridge. The shortened funnels improved her appearance and made her look more modern, so that she was at her best and smartest during her last years.

Old ships, however, cannot last forever. In April 1955 *Prince Rupert* was laid up for the last time at the Canadian National Dock in Vancouver. She was now 45 years old. The freight and passenger service to Prince Rupert and northern ports was also nearing its end, outdated by new roads and air services. Canadian National and Canadian Pacific agreed to operate a joint service, to be maintained by the C.P.R.'s *Princess Norah* of 1928.

In order that neither company should be unduly favored, in 1955 she was renamed *Queen of the North* and given a non-partisan blue funnel with a black top. The crew was provided by Canadian Pacific which continued to own and operate the ship, but silver, linen, and other furnishing were supplied by Canadian National. This arrangement continued until the autumn of 1957. Next year she was sold to Northland Navigation Company of Vancouver and renamed *Canadian Prince*. She continued to sail on the northern route until 1964 when she lost her mail subsidy with a change of government in Ottawa. She was then sold to become a floating restaurant at Kodiak, Alaska, under the name *Beach-comber*. So ended the traditional service to Prince Rupert started over half a century previously by the *Rupert City* in 1908.

The demise of the *Prince Rupert* came in June 1956 when she was sold to Japan for scrapping. At the time I made a rather sad tour of the old ship as she lay boarded up for her last voyage and wrote:

"There is a heavy pall of dust and soot everywhere. Carpets have been torn up and cabins stripped, and the only furniture remaining is a few chairs under dust covers. Mirrors are heavy with grit and the old-fashioned panelling that looked so smart in 1910 looks distressly shabby.

"In the wheelhouse the brass telegraphs which once shone so brightly are a dull green. The wooden steering wheel is still bright, polished by the hands of her many quartermasters.

"Soon the *Prince Rupert* will be no more, victim of old age, and changing habits of transportation."

The old ship was renamed *Prince Maru* by her new owners, a delivery crew was sent out from Japan, and her engines, idle for a year, were revved up for her final sad voyage. As if they were loath to leave Burrard Inlet for the last time, they broke down three times as she left the harbour. But once initial problems were corrected, the *Prince Maru* sailed out into the Pacific with a crew of 35 to reach her destiny in a Japanese scrap yard.

Now only the second *Prince George* was available to carry on Canadian National's Pacific coast service, and even she limited her sailings to tourist cruises to Alaska. In the spring of 1975 she was 28 years old, expensive to operate with her outdated Uniflow steam power. In the spring of that year the company announced officially that she would be withdrawn from service at the end of that season.

It was not to be. On April 10, six weeks prior

to the first scheduled sailing, a fire broke out on board while she lay alongside the dock at Vancouver. The damage involved 20 staterooms and it was estimated that repairs would cost $400,000. In view of this situation Canadian National cancelled the final cruise season and put the ship up for sale.

After four months of lay-up she was purchased by the British Columbia Steamship Company, owned by the provincial government, which already operated the former Canadian Pacific *Princess Marguerite* in a summer service between Victoria and Seattle. The final cost amounted to $230,000, plus 28 acres of provincial government land beside the C.N. rail yards in the city of Prince George.

The B.C. Steamship Company announced plans to operate *Prince George* on weekly round trips along the B.C. coast during the 1976 tourist season. Then a change of government resulted in a change of plans. In March 1976 she was sold to Wong Brothers Enterprises Ltd. of Nanaimo for $325,000, who announced plans to use her as a floating restaurant and convention centre. She was towed to Nanaimo from Victoria in May 1976 and there she lay idle, her new owners apparently short of funds. Later she spent six months at Port Angeles where she served as an accommodation ship for management personnel during a strike at the Rayonier pulp mill. Then followed a bewildering series of ownerships. Early in 1979 she was reported sold to Yong Management Ltd. of Vancouver.

In April 1979 she left Victoria in tow for Portland, Oregon, where it was reported that she had been sold to Luka Holdings. She lay idle alongside a pier in the Willamette River until she was towed back in January 1981, the new owners having apparently defaulted on their payments. She was again registered under the ownership of Wong Brothers until she was purchased by a syndicate of Victoria physicians who registered her under the name of Canadian Cruise Lines Ltd. They announced they would spend $4 million on a refit so she could return to the Alaska cruise trade. The actual refit cost $495,000. On her first cruise out of Vancouver with passengers, her engines broke down in the Gulf Islands and she had to return to port. Wherever she went she left behind a black plume, and she was twice charged at Juneau for making excess smoke.

Another attempt was made to enter the Alaska cruise trade in 1982 by a new syndicate called Canadian Cruise Lines (1982), but the poor old ship continued to trail a cloud of smoke and financial losses. Two of her scheduled cruises were dropped because of engine trouble. Eventually, she was seized by the Continental Bank of Canada and laid up at Vancouver. Subsequent owners in 1985 were Ponderosa Venture, Inc., and Southport Associates. In 1988 she was arrested for $10,000 moorage fees owing to Versatile Pacific Shipyard.

The next owner was Unicorn Enterprises Ltd., who found a job for her. On May 21, 1989, she was towed to Valdez, Alaska, to act as an accommodation ship for workmen engaged in the *Exxon Valdez* cleanup. She returned south on November 4. The next announcement was that she was to become a mining museum berthed at Britannia Beach in Howe Sound. There she has remained ever since, with only a watchman aboard. Her last owner was said to be Limbourg Investments Ltd., of Jersey, Channel Islands.

Her latter days have been a sad climax to the last surviving ship of a once proud coastwise passenger shipping company.

CHAPTER NINE

End of an Era

After the withdrawal of the Union Steamship Company from the northern runs, the subsidized services to Prince Rupert and Stewart were taken over by the Northland Navigation Com-

pany Ltd. of Vancouver. In 1963 they took delivery of a new passenger-freighter for the run. She was launched at Burrard Dry Dock as *Northland Prince*, 329 feet long, with accommodation for 120 passengers. She had her engines aft, and was no beauty, but with her large freight capacity, she was a practical and economical vessel, and proved very successful on the run. She was 3,150 tons gross, and was powered by a 4,200 h.p. Stork diesel.

Northland Navigation Company Ltd. had been founded in a small way in 1942 by Captain H. J. C. Terry with a single wooden freighter, the *Island Prince*, as the British Columbia Steamship Company Ltd. The company was re-

B.C. Ferries' *Queen of the North*, below, continues the service between Prince Rupert and Vancouver Island which started in 1966 with the *Queen of Prince*

Rupert. Three years previously the Alaska Marine System's *Malaspina*, opposite page, had started a service from Prince Rupert to Alaska.

named Northland in 1952 and grew rapidly. It took over the C.P.R. service on the west coast of Vancouver Island in 1958 and next year absorbed the pioneer Union Steamship Company of British Columbia, Ltd., founded in 1889. All its ships were given the "Prince" suffix, thus maintaining the old Grand Trunk Pacific tradition.

But *Northland Prince* also fell victim to political interference. She lost her subsidy in 1976 and Northland withdrew all its passenger services on the coast, providing only tug and barge facilities. This withdrawal left a big gap, with outports such as Ocean Falls and the Queen Charlotte Islands without adequate communication with the south. Northland Navigation Company had meanwhile been acquired by the Van

Ommeren interests of Holland. After a few years, however, the Dutch company gave up the struggle and withdrew from British Columbia.

The subsequent career of *Northland Prince* took her far away from her native shores. In 1977 she was sold to the government of the island of St. Helena, in the South Atlantic, famed for the exile there of Napoleon Bonaparte. The Island had been cut off from its traditional mail and passenger service by the Union-Castle Line, and so a substitute had to be found. *Northland Prince* proved ideal for the trade. Renamed R.M.S. *St. Helena*, she gave regular liner sailings from Southampton to the Island, with a southern terminus at Cape Town. Passenger accommodation was then about 90. During the Falkland Islands campaign in 1982

she was requisitioned by the British Admiralty for service in the war zone as a minesweeper depot ship.

By 1989 she was showing her age, and a new ship was ordered to replace her, also called *St. Helena*. After a brief renaming as *St. Helena Island* in 1990, the former *Northland Prince* was sold to a Maltese firm called Sea Safaris Ltd. She was renamed *Avalon* and put on a new cruise service between Durban and the Seychelles. This service proved unsuccessful and she was sold at auction at Durban for $215,000, aged 31. In 1993 she was purchased by Indoceanic Maritime Enterprises Ltd. of the island of Mauritius and renamed *Indoceanique*.

The city of Prince Rupert was given a new sea connection with the outside world in 1966 when the ferry *Queen of Prince Rupert* was launched for the British Columbia Ferry Authority by the Victoria Machinery Depot. She is a vessel of 5,864 gross tons, 332 feet long, with a service speed of 18 knots. She has a capacity for 80 cars and 458 passengers, with stateroom accommodation for many of them.

She began service to Prince Rupert in 1966, sailing out of the ferry terminal at Tsawwassen. As roads were built up the east coast of Vancouver Island, her southern terminal was extended to Kelsey Bay and later to Port Hardy. In 1980 she was placed on the daylight summer run between Victoria and Seattle to replace the popular *Princess Marguerite* and briefly renamed *Victoria Princess*. She was not a success, and the ageing "*Maggie*" was recalled.

In 1974 the B.C. Ferry Authority had purchased the Baltic ferry *Stena Danica* and renamed her *Queen of Surrey* for service between Tsawwassen and Swartz Bay on Vancouver Island. She is a fine vessel with extensive overnight accommodation, but proved unsuitable for the short run in the Strait of Georgia. Built in

1969 for service between Sweden and Denmark, she is 410 feet long overall, with a service speed of 22 knots. In 1980 the Ferry authority decided to place her on the more suitable run between Port Hardy and Prince Rupert, and she was sent to the Burrard-Yarrows shipyard in Vancouver for a $7.5 million refit. At a dockside ceremony at Prince Rupert on March 30, 1980, she was officially renamed *Queen of the North*, second vessel of that name on the northern route. She is 8,889 tons gross and accommodates 750 passengers and 157 cars. *Queen of Prince Rupert*, after her failure on the Seattle run, was placed on service between Prince Rupert and Skidegate, with two trips a week in the summer.

Meanwhile, Prince Rupert had received another ferry service. In February 1963, the state of Alaska inaugurated the Alaska Marine System with the new Seattle-built *Malaspina*, operating via way points, Seattle to Skagway, 525 miles north. The 408-foot vessel was lengthened by 56 feet in 1972 and now has 284 first-class berths.

The Alaska Ferry System was less successful with their original plans to operate a deluxe ferry between Seattle and Alaska. In 1968 they purchased the *Stena Britannica* from the Stena Line of Sweden, built in 1967 to run between Great Britain and France. She was a fine ship. 5,300 tons, similar to the *Stena Danica*. Incredibly, the Alaskans forgot one important factor. Under the restrictive Jones Act legislation, only American-built ships can carry passengers between two American ports. So the grand new ferry, which was renamed *Wickersham* under the flag of Panama, was forced to operate out of Vancouver, and later out of Prince Rupert, to southeastern Alaska ports. This schedule was obviously unsatisfactory, so the ship was sold at a loss in 1974. She returned to the Baltic for further service under the Finnish flag. She was replaced by a new American-built ferry, the *Columbia*, which now operates out of Bellingham to Alaska ports, with summer calls at Prince Rupert.

And what about the original community of Prince Rupert during the steamship era? After the end of the Second World War the city began to wake up from its long slumbers and to realize some of the dreams and ambitions of Charles Melville Hays. It has never reached his projected population of 50,000, but it is no longer a raw western outpost of muskeg, rocks and rain. There is still plenty of rain, but it is now a well built and handsome little city, with new industries and thriving port facilities.

The floating dry dock is gone. It could never pay its way, for after the wartime shipbuilding boom, business vanished. In 1951 it was put up for sale by the War Assets Corporation, and three years later was sold to Puget Sound Bridge and Dredging Company of Seattle. It was towed to Seattle in January 1955.

The first new industry to arrive in Prince Rupert after the war was a pulp mill established at the nearby suburb of Port Edward by Columbia Cellulose Company. It occupies the site of a huge warehouse built by the U.S. Army during the wartime emergency. Then the dream of Charles Hays to create a great national port began to come to fruition. In 1972 Ottawa designated the port of Prince Rupert as a national harbour, with local administration established under the control of the National Harbours Board.

Hays had forseen the day when prairie grain and Peace River coal would be shipping out of Prince Rupert, which is a day and half closer to key markets of the Orient than any other port on the West Coast. It also has the most northerly transcontinental railhead. A new general cargo facility was built at Fairview, west of the downtown area, in 1977, and a major expansion finished in 1990. In 1981 construction began on the $750 million Ridley Island coal and grain shipping facilities close to Port Edward. The grain elevator was built by a consortium of prairie grain exporters, with China its chief market.

On March 11, 1985, the 250,000-ton bulk freighter *World Prize* went under the spouts of the new terminal and loaded the first cargo of wheat. The elevator has a storage capacity of 200,000 tons.

After a deal was made with Japanese coal importers, the Tumbler Ridge coalfields in the Peace River area were developed. This project included building a railway line from Tumbler Ridge to connect with the Canadian National at Prince George. On January 9, 1984, the first coal cargo to Japan was shipped from the Ridley Island terminal.

In addition to kraft pulp, wheat and coal, Prince Rupert ships lumber from the B.C. Interior, ore concentrates and sulphur. The port also has a growing and extensive tourist industry, as it benefits from the operations of both the British Columbia Ferry Corporation and the Alaska Marine Highway System. It is also a base for cruise ships carrying tourists north to view the glaciers and fjords of the Alaska Panhandle, and is the terminus of transcontinental Highway 16 which winds its way down the scenic gorges of the Skeena River.

The beautiful and efficient Prince ships of the early days are gone, but Prince Rupert now benefits from the potential attractions foreseen nearly a century ago by C. M. Hays. He wasn't wrong. He was just premature.

Bibliography

Affleck, Edward L. "Affleck's List of Sternwheelers Plying the Inland Waters of British Columbia." Vancouver, 1963.

Bailey, Ruth Greene. "Canadian National Steamships Historic Steamer *Prince Rupert*." Harbour & Shipping, Vancouver. August 1973.

Bowman, Phylis. "Steaming Through Northern Waters." Port Edward, B.C. 1987.

Bowman, Phylis. "Muskeg, Rocks and Rain!" Port Edward, B.C. 1973.

Clapp, Frank A. "Canadian National Ferry *Canora*." Steamboat Bill. Fall 1969.

Clapp, Frank A. "Mackenzie Brothers Ltd., Steamship Owners and Operators, Vancouver B.C." The Sea Chest, Seattle, September-December 1994.

Cooke, Anthony. "Emigrant Ships." Carmania Press. London. n.d.

Dalzell, Kathleen E. "The Queen Charlotte Islands." Terrace, B.C. 1968.

Eisele, Peter T. "Grimaldi-Siosa Story." Steamboat Bill. Spring 1985.

Gibbs, Jim. "Disaster Log of Ships." Seattle. 1961.

Hacking, Norman, and Lamb, W. Kaye. "The Princess Story: A Century and a Half of West Coast Shipping." Vancouver. 1974

Henderson, John D. "Saint Class Tugs Under the Canadian Flag 1923-1983." Steamboat Bill. Spring 1992.

Isherwood, John H. "Grand Trunk Pacific Liner *Prince Rupert* of 1910." Sea Breezes. January 1962.

Isherwood, John H. "Canadian National *Prince Henry* of 1930." Sea Breezes. September 1983.

Large, R. Geddes. "The Skeena: River of Destiny." Vancouver. 1957.

Large, R.G. "Prince Rupert: A Gateway to Alaska." Vancouver. 1960.

Mathers, Agnes C. "Memories of the *Prince John*." Tales from the Queen Charlotte Islands. Masset, B.C. 1979.

Menard, Allan A. "Brief History of Canadian National Steamships on Canada's West Coast." m.s. Vancouver. 1975.

Murphy, Gavin. "Canada's Forgotten Railway Tycoon." The Beaver. December 1993.

Newell, Gordon, ed. "The H. W. McCurdy Marine History of the Pacific Northwest." Seattle, 1966.

Ommundsen, Peter. "*Prince George*. Last Days With Canadian National." Steamboat Bill. Fall 1976.

O'Neill, Wiggs. "Steamboat Days on the Skeena River." Smithers, B.C. 1960.

Rogers, Fred. "Shipwrecks of British Columbia." Vancouver. 1973.

Rogers, Fred. "More Shipwrecks of British Columbia." Vancouver. 1992.

Rushton, Gerald. "Whistle Up The Inlet." Vancouver. 1974.

Saul, Lieut.-Cmdr. A. M. Kinnersley, R.N.R. "Naval War on B.C. Coast Had Series of Humorous Features." Vancouver Daily Province. 3 March 1934. Reprinted from "The Navy." February 1934.

Schull, Joseph. "The Far Distant Ships." Ottawa. 1961.

Taylor, G. W. "Shipyards of British Columbia: The Principal Companies." Victoria, B.C. 1986.

Tucker, Gilbert Norman. "The Naval Service of Canada. Vol. 2." Ottawa. 1952.

Turner, Robert D. "The Pacific Princesses." Victoria, B.C. 1977.

Webb, Robert Lloyd. "On the Northwest: Commerical Whaling in the Pacific Northwest 1790-1967." Vancouver. 1988.

Wicks, Walter. "Memories of the Skeena." Saanichton, B.C. 1976.

"Canadian National Steamships Ltd." Canadian Merchant Service Guild Annual. Vancouver. 1930.

Index

INDEX Ships